For Jimmy
Happy Birthday
Love
Jan Daniel
Mia & Phillips Silas

America's
Natural Beauty

America's
Natural Beauty

Philip N. Steele

Crescent Books
New York

Photographic acknowledgments
Alabama Bureau of Travel and Tourism, 81 bottom; State of Alaska, Division
of Tourism, 240, 241; Ardea, London, 110, 111 bottom, 114, 115, 119 top, 175
bottom, 185 top, 234, 235; Arkansas Department of Parks and Tourism, 82,
83; Heather Angel, Biofotos, Surrey, 144 bottom, 219 bottom, 223, 242–243;
Tom Bean, Arizona, 132 top, 136–137, 139 bottom, 142 top, 224, 225, 232,
239 bottom; Click-Chicago, Illinois, 85, 87, 89, 91, 92, 93, 100, 101, 103, 104,
105, 106, 109, 117 bottom; Bruce Coleman, Uxbridge, 10, 35 bottom, 36, 37,
113, 131 bottom, 148–149, 175 top, 211, 212, 213, 220 top, 247; Michael Dent,
East Twickenham, 194 bottom, 206–207; Florida Department of Commerce,
Division of Tourism, 72; Robert Harding, London, 130; International Stock
Photography, New York, 13, 19, 20, 21, 23, 25, 26, 27, 30, 32, 33, 34 bottom,
35 top, 39, 42, 43, 44, 45, 46, 47, 50, 55 top, 55 bottom, 57 bottom, 59, 61, 62,
63, 66, 67, 69, 77, 78, 80, 81, 94, 95, 96, 97, 102, 108, 123, 126 bottom, 132–
133 bottom, 133 top, 134 bottom, 135, 138, 139 top, 143 top, 152, 153, 159
bottom, 162 bottom, 163, 164, 165, 166 top, 167, 168, 169 bottom, 172, 173,
177 bottom, 179 bottom, 181 top, 188, 189, 191, 192, 193, 195, 196, 197
bottom, 198, 199, 205, 208, 209, 210, 211, 215, 217 top, 218, 220 bottom, 221,
222, 226, 227, 242; Frank Lane Picture Agency, London, 7 top, 11, 28, 34 top,
51, 54, 68 top, 68 bottom, 79, 81 top, 84, 90, 107, 111 bottom, 119 bottom,
127 top, 145 top, 147, 156, 176, 177, 186, 187, 201 top, 219, 228, 229, 231, 236,
237, 238, 239, 244, 245; Louisiana Office of Tourism, 83; Nevada Commission
of Tourism, 202; Oxford Scientific Films, Oxford, 70–71, 184 bottom, 233;
David Parker, London, 150, 151, 154, 155 bottom, 157, 159 top, 160, 161;
Rhode Island Department of Economic Development, 29; The Photo Source,
London, 140, 141, 170, 171, 216; St. Croix National Scenic Riverway,
Wisconsin, Minnesota, 99; Seaphot/Planet Earth Pictures, London, 73, 74, 75;
Spectrum Colour Library, London, 53; Texas Tourist Development Agency,
118 top, 120–121, 122 bottom, 124–125; United States Department of
Agriculture: Allegheny National Forest, 40, 41; Monongahela National
Forest, West Virginia, 15, 50; United States Department of the Interior,
National Park Service: Capitol Reef National Park, Utah, 158; Congaree
Swamp National Monument, South Carolina, 65; Crater Lake National Park
(NP), California, 200; Lassen Volcanic NP, California, 204, 205; Mammouth
Cave NP, Kentucky, 56, 57 top; Mesa Verde NP, Colorado, 171; North
Dakota National Parks Service, 112; Sequoia and Kings Canyon NP,
California, 214, 216, 217 bottom; West Virginia Natonal Parks Service, 48, 49;
Yellowstone NP, Wyoming, 179 top; Vision International, London, 7 bottom,
8–9, 17, 58, 76, 110 top, 182–183, 213, 128–129 bottom, 129 top, 246, 248–
249, Wisconsin Division of Tourism, 98; Wyoming Travel Commission, 180.

Front cover: Fall, Adirondack Mountains, New York State
       (Image Bank, London)
Back cover: Grand Canyon National Park, Arizona
       (International Stock Photography, New York)
Title spread: Merced River, Yellowstone National Park, Wyoming
       (Vision International, London)
Endpapers: Hayden Valley, Yellowstone National Park, Wyoming
       (Alan Hutchison Library, London)

First English edition published by Newnes Books
Bridge House, Twickenham, Middlesex

Prepared by Deans International Publishing
A division of The Hamlyn Publishing Group Limited
London·New York·Sydney·Toronto

This 1986 edition is published by Crescent Books
Distributed by Crown Publishers, Inc.

ISBN 0-517-49640-2
h g f e d c b a

Printed in Spain

Contents

Introduction

How canst thou walk these streets, who has trod the green turf of the prairies?
How canst thou breathe this air, who hast breathed the sweet air of the mountains?

Henry Wadsworth Longfellow (1807–82)

Right top: Big Cypress National Preserve is part of the complex wetland system of Florida, together with the Everglades. This wilderness of cypress and swamp was formerly hunted by the Miccosukee and Seminole Indians.

In his poem *To the Driving Cloud* Longfellow addresses the "chief of the mighty Omahas" and expresses the sense of loss experienced by a poet whose generation had felled the great forests of the North American continent for railroad ties, tamed the Wild West, and filled the eastern skies with the smoke of their factory chimneys. The first European settlers of America were fascinated by the wilderness and the wide open spaces. Many of today's visitors to the U.S.A. have been attracted rather by the romance of the great cities, by television and film accounts of Los Angeles and New York City. Many Americans, too, become so involved in the cut and thrust of urban life that they forget that much of the wilderness and virgin forest remains unspoiled, that a world awaits them where peace and beauty remain unchallenged.

One perhaps unexpected result of the space age is that human beings, as much as looking outwards to the mysteries of the solar system, have for the first time been looking back at their own planet. When one examines a satellite photograph of earth, one experiences the same shock as a primitive man must have felt on first gazing into a mirror. The maps in one's school atlas could scarcely do justice to the majestic coastline of North America, set in blue seas and wreathed in white clouds. The cameras close in on details. Here is the arctic tundra of Alaska; there is the great Columbia River, snaking westward. Coloration techniques reveal surface features: forests, prairies, rock formations. This overall view makes it easier to understand inter-relationships between town and country, between climate and landscape, vegetation and wildlife. The scale seems to emphasize the fragility of the ecological balance and the temporality of geological formation. It makes it easier to envisage the prehistoric drift of the continents and shifts in the plates that form the earth's crust.

With one's feet on terra firma it is easy to assume that the landscapes we are looking at and the climate we experience today are eternal constants. Nothing of course could be further from the truth: The landscape is dynamic, not static, perpetually restructured by elemental forces. In prehistoric times lush swamps covered what are now barren deserts, and many of today's mountain peaks were once the beds of inland seas. Periodic convulsions of the crust throw up mighty ranges such as the Rockies. These are then ground down by ice, washed by rain, and cracked by heat and frost; they are blasted by wind and sand until they are rounded, gentle slopes like the eastern Appalachians. Erosion is such a slow process, it outlasts countless generations. One day the Niagara Falls themselves will cease to flow, but only in a distant future one can barely comprehend. In other places, silting and sediment are building up new coastlines. The effects of these timeless geological processes are all around us, in the plunging chasm of the Grand Canyon, in the rugged Badlands of the Dakotas, in the shifting dunes of the

Right bottom: Utah, a land of visions and visionaries, in which natural rock formations rival the human imagination. Here, Delicate Arch frames the mountainous landscape of the Arches National Park, in the west of the state.

The extraordinary expanse of Bryce Canyon National Park, in Garfield and Kane Counties, Utah. The eroded pinnacles of rock rise like fangs to the horizon. The Pink Cliffs are part of a series of giant steps – eroded strata of rock – descending to the Kaibab Plateau and the Grand Canyon.

Atlantic seaboard. Sometimes erosion reveals the fossilized remains of strange creatures from another era, sea creatures or dinosaurs like the dragons of mythology, and we are suddenly confronted with our own latterday place in the scheme of things. Sometimes evidence of the earth's restlessness is brought home to us more forcibly, in a sudden terrifying lurch along the San Andreas Fault, or in a volcanic eruption such as that which devastated Mount St. Helens in 1980. It is this mutability which is part of our fascination for the great canyons and peaks and natural monuments of North America, for here we are forced to measure ourselves against eternity.

If the landscape is subject to constant change over the millennia, one might be tempted to question the aims of the conservationists. Surely, if a state of flux is inevitable, it is futile to attempt to stop this natural process. Why conserve endangered wildlife species such as the whooping crane when natural selection shows no compassion? After all, the landscape and its vegetation has changed many times, and countless species became extinct long before *homo sapiens* arrived on the scene. Such misgivings are misconceived. The purpose of conservation is not to prevent change, but to respond effectively to humanity's rapidly increasing capacity for destruction. Human beings have speeded up the wheels of change to the point where nature might blow a fuse. Humans have forgotten that they too are a constituent part of the ecosystem, dependent upon it for their own survival. The American landscape has been populated for a miniscule part of its history; during the last 150 years, an infinitesimal part of that period, the effects of human settlement on the American landscape have been traumatic indeed.

North America was unpopulated until about 50,000 years ago, when Asian peoples migrated to Alaska from Siberia across the Bering land bridge. They hunted the mammals of the Ice Age, such as the mammoth. Their descendants spread the length and breadth of the Americas, living

Niagara: One of the world's most famous waterfalls. Capping rock below this passage between Lakes Ontario and Erie is constantly undermined by erosion of the underlying shale, and so the cliff edge is broken down. Such gradual processes are not evident within human lifespans. To visitors, the thundering torrent seems both transitory and eternal at the same time, a unique experience.

In a gentle mood: Vegetation takes over at the edge of Colorado's Great Sand Dunes National Monument. The peaks of the Sangre de Cristo chain gleam in the pale sunshine.

off the bounty of the land. Later immigrants from Asia were the Eskimo or Inuit peoples, who settled the inhospitable Arctic. In time, many of these people developed flourishing cultures. In the pre-Columbian period architectural skills were demonstrated at Mesa Verde in Colorado and other sites in the southwest. Agriculture was practiced in some areas of North America; in other places people continued to live by hunting animals or gathering roots and berries. At no point did this way of life threaten the environment. The technology was not available for large-scale destruction of the habitat, and anyway the philosophy of the American Indian peoples was largely one of respect for nature.

The same was not true of the European settlers. The first landfalls of the Vikings were to be followed by Christopher Columbus' Bahamas landing in 1492. In 1513 the Spaniards reached Florida, founding the colony of St. Augustine in 1565. The French penetrated the Great Lakes region and followed the Mississippi southward. The British had occupied the eastern seaboard, and by 1760 they had 13 colonies. Plantations of cotton and tobacco covered the southeastern states, worked by black slaves imported from Africa under inhumane conditions. The Indians, initially friendly toward the colonists, were harassed, cheated, and removed from their ancestral lands by force.

The first settlers cleared virgin forest with their axes. Their descendants, and the immigrants who flooded into the newly independent country during the nineteenth century, saw the land as something wild they had to wrestle with and tame. They wished to leave their mark on the land, to exploit its resources to the hilt, to possess it. Prospectors staked their claim to western wildernesses, lured on by the glint of gold or silver. In the east, the downtrodden of Europe came to seek their fortune, and cities and factories spilled across the countryside. To many nineteenth-century Americans the ideal was one of progress toward some technological golden age in which materialism was tempered only by religiosity. The natural heritage of America was the sacrificial lamb.

Admittedly, the romantic movement in the arts had aroused a popular interest in the more beautiful scenery of the United States, and the railroad, and later the internal combustion engine, had brought the backwoods within reach of the common man and woman for the first time. From New York City, early tourists traveled upstate to visit Niagara Falls. The wealthier traveled west to marvel at Yosemite. Too often, however, natural beauty was sentimentalized and commercialized. It was viewed rather as one might a wild animal in a menagerie, and a mawkish sense of the picturesque was insufficient to prevent further despoliation of the natural heritage. The huge herds of bison were decimated. The passenger pigeon, once one of the country's more common bird species, had been completely exterminated in the wild by the turn of the century. Deforestation and over-intensive agricultural methods led to the creation of dustbowls.

Like most golden ages, the technological dreams of the nineteenth century failed to materialize. Technology advanced, to be sure, but it was certainly no cure-all for human problems. The misery of dustbowl farmers in our own century brought it home to many that conservation of the landscape was not merely romantic wishful thinking, but a practical necessity. The land was there for us to nurture, not to rape. A polluted atmosphere and poisoned rivers served nobody's interest. The habitat, animals, and plants had to survive alongside human beings, automobiles, and concrete, for they were the nation's most precious asset. Government agencies became actively involved in the fight to manage its resources in a wiser manner. In 1872 the first national park had been established, at Yellowstone in wild Wyoming. Yosemite, the most magical valley in California, followed in 1890. An ardent campaigner on behalf of Yosemite was John Muir, the father of the movement to conserve the American landscape. A close acquaintance of Muir's was Gifford Pinchot, who developed new ideas of forestry

management which allowed for controlled exploitation. Political will and muscle combined in the figure of Theodore Roosevelt (1858–1919), who succeeded to the presidency of the United States in 1901. A hunter and a rancher, Roosevelt was a lover of the great outdoors and a tireless campaigner for federal land protection. The Forest Reserve Act of 1891 provided a stepping stone for the creation during Roosevelt's term of office of millions of acres of national forestland. During the twentieth century, the forests began to spring up once again over much of the ravaged landscape of the eastern states. The American people began to evaluate how much country remained unspoiled. They explored the rapidly burgeoning national park system with the same sense of wonder as the early pioneers.

The fight to preserve the North American landscape is by no means over. Take one kind of habitat as an example: the wetlands. The U.S. Fish and Wildlife Service estimates that 11 million acres of vegetated wetlands disappeared from the mid-1950s to the mid-1970s, largely because of agricultural drainage or coastal dredging. Wetlands play a vital part in the national ecological framework, as the home of myriad wild animals and plants. They include some of the nation's finest scenery, and are valuable recreational areas. As if this were not enough, the survival of the wetlands ensures the production of fish and timber. They act as a safety valve at the time of floods, and protect the coast by absorbing the force of oncoming storms. The wetlands *must* be protected and conserved.

Many agencies, some state-run, some federal, some commercial, are engaged in today's drive to preserve the American heritage. The National Forest Service manages 115 forests and 19 grasslands over 191 million acres of land. This takes in much of the most magnificent landscape in the continent, stretching from Alaska to Florida. National forests include 25.3 million acres designated as wilderness. The practical aim of the service is to manage both commercial timber production and natural forests, to combat soil erosion, create watersheds, and sustain animal life. Here above all is a chance to experience nature at first hand, riding or hiking the 100,000 miles of forest trails. There are 6,000 camping

Overleaf: The big freeze in West Virginia's Monongahela National Forest: Winters in the Appalachians can be severe. This forest covers the mountain slopes south of the Maryland line, returning these much abused hills to their former glory.

grounds and picnic sites, and all kinds of recreational facilities.

The 56 national parks cover about half as much land as the national forests and include nearly all the most scenic areas of the U.S.A., from the Everglades to Grand Teton. No visit to the United States is complete without a visit to at least one or two national parks, for preserved in these deserts, mountains, and forests is the true heart of America. Here, too, are boundless opportunities for outdoor pursuits and exploration. Such has been the growth of interest in the beauties of the backwoods that in some places the sheer volume of visitors is itself a threat to the environment. Walkers can wear out a mountain. This should be borne in mind when planning a visit to a national park: Avoid the most populated trails, and obey the regulations – they have been drawn up for good reasons. The most remote and some of the most splendid parks are on a truly gigantic scale. The Gates of the Arctic National Park alone covers more than 8½ million acres of Alaska. The National Park Service also manages a variety of national monuments, which include many beauty spots as well as sites of historic interest. Other specially designated areas include national rivers, lakeshores, seashores, preserves, and recreation areas, many of which are featured in this book. Further tracts of terrain are under the control of the Bureau of Land Management, who grant public access to many of the most beautiful and interesting areas.

The first national wildlife refuge was founded in 1903, on Pelican Island in Florida. Today there are over 400 refuges across 49 states and five trust territories. The largest is to be found in Alaska, where over 19½ million acres of the Yukon Delta have been set aside for the bird life of the region. The refuges also harbor some 60 species which have become endangered, and protect the long north-south migratory routes of millions of birds. The refuges also welcome human visitors, some 27 million passing through each year.

The best way to explore the American landscape depends upon the locality and the individual. The tundra and peaks of Alaska are best viewed from a light aircraft, while the lakes of Minnesota's Voyageurs National Park may be crossed in more traditional manner – by canoe. One can ski through the Tetons in winter, or ride a mule down the cliffs of the Grand Canyon. Most visitors travel by car or bus and many national parks offer spectacular overlooks and scenic drives. Campers are especially well catered for in the United States with forest and park campgrounds to suit every taste, from the primitive to the most developed. More and more visitors choose to explore the American landscape on foot, hiking along the profusion of well-marked trails. This is probably the most rewarding way in which to get to know the countryside, experiencing the elements and observing the plants and wild creatures. Conditions can be tough: Backpackers should prepare themselves thoroughly and gain experience by stages. In many places, permits will be required for camping backcountry. The nation is crossed by three "supertrails:" the Pacific Crest National Scenic Trail, which follows the western peaks southward; the Continental Divide National Scenic Trail; and the Appalachian National Scenic Trail, in the east.

No other nation in the world takes in such a variety of climatic conditions and vegetation zones. In the U.S.A. one can watch huge glaciers breaking off into arctic seas, and long-snouted alligators sliding through subtropical swamps; one can see the fragile blossoms of the Hawaiian Islands, and the spiny cactuses of the Sonoran Desert. In the world's most developed nation, there are still wolves and eagles and grizzly bears: America is full of surprises. To a visitor from another country the first impression is one of vastness. The huge distances are traveled with some desperation, by flying or driving thousands of miles. Perhaps it is better to slow down, to travel rather at the pace of the covered wagons which took settlers westward along the Oregon Trail in the last century. In this way one can truly appreciate the natural heritage of America, and come to know it and care for it. Care and increased understanding are the key to its survival. Its future is in your hands.

Cathedral Spires in Yosemite National Park, California, a majestic rampart of rock high above the Merced River. It was such views that inspired John Muir to campaign for a national park around the Yosemite Valley. The modern national park contains 750 miles of trails and attracts hikers, climbers, and natural history enthusiasts. Thirty-seven different kinds of tree are to be found in the park and some 1,200 species of flowering plant.

The Northeast

Connecticut, Delaware, Maine, Maryland,
Massachusetts, New Hampshire, New Jersey,
New York, Pennsylvania, Rhode Island, Vermont,
West Virginia; District of Columbia

Imagine how the first European settlers must have felt, disembarking
from their tiny wooden ships in some rocky cove. After weeks of salt-
laden gales and poor food, they were now splashing ashore on the edge of
an unknown wilderness. They had made a decision of frightening
finality: to leave behind the cosy fishing villages of Devon or Brittany, or
the bustling streets of Amsterdam or London. With the passing of the
centuries the term "New World" has become stale through familiarity,
but a new world it was, in every sense – a revelation that accorded well
with the early settlers' visionary religious faith. To the native Amerindian
peoples, however, it was by now an old world, but nonetheless an
awesome one.

The *Mayflower* was one of these tiny ships, its passengers were
Puritans sailing from Plymouth, England, to escape religious
persecution. In 1620, battered by storms, they landed at Cape Cod. The
rest is history. In 1626 Dutch colonists purchased Manhattan from the
Indians, to found New Amsterdam, later New York. To the south,
English and Welsh Quakers under William Penn founded the colony of
Pennsylvania in 1682. As English colonies developed along the coast, the
initially friendly Indian tribes were repeatedly attacked and dispersed. In
the conflict, the eastern seaboard became the crucible of a new nation,
which found its identity in the War of Independence against Great
Britain. In the nineteenth century it was the Northeast that came to
preeminence, its dominant position confirmed by victory over the
Confederacy in 1865 and by successful expansion westward. The
landscape, already cleared for agriculture by the axes of the first settlers,
now spewed forth factories, mines and large centers of population,
swelled by an influx of immigrants from a troubled Europe. The
twentieth century saw the northeastern states become the powerhouse of
the world's most dynamic and powerful nation. Today that power is
more widely dispersed: In the West, California alone could happily run
its own affairs as an independent nation. Even so, the Northeast, from
Washington D.C. to New York City, remains the focal point of the
United States.

The Northeast found favor because of its geographical location on the
Atlantic shipping routes, because of its temperate climate, its rich
agricultural possibilities, and its natural resources. Stretching southward
from Maine, the coast forms a ragged hook like the pincer of a lobster at
Cape Cod. Manhattan Island, a sliver of land between the Hudson and
the East rivers, leads to Long Island, which reaches out into the open
Atlantic. The New Jersey coastline, with its barrier islands, stretches
south to Cape May and Delaware Bay. Between the mouths of the
Delaware and the Susquehanna rivers, the long peninsula encloses
Chesapeake Bay and the Potomac Estuary. Inland, the Appalachian
chain forms a long spine from New England southward, extending all the
way to Georgia. This mountain system includes the Alleghenies, which

A coastal drive on Maine's Mount Desert Island reveals forests, pebble beaches, and rocky shores. Once lying within the French territory of Acadie, the island now forms the largest unit of the Acadia National Park.

straddle Pennsylvania and West Virginia, the latter state being bounded to the west by the Ohio River. The shores of New York State are washed in the west by the waters of Lake Erie and Lake Ontario, on the Canadian border.

The northeastern states are the most populated in the entire country. In 1980 New England averaged 196 people per square mile; New York, 370.6; New Jersey, 986.2. The federal District of Columbia, site of Washington, the nation's capital, averaged an incredible 10,132.3 in the same year. The comparable figures for Wyoming are 4.8 and for Alaska 0.7. When Europeans first encroached upon the North American continent, it is thought that under 2 million people were already living there. Today, three or four times as many live in New York City alone. It is hardly surprising that such a history of settlement and industrialization has taken its toll on the landscape and the environment. What is perhaps surprising is that the Northeast has retained so many of its natural features, its colorful woodland and its rocky shores, its native flora and fauna.

The state of Maine is a prime example. Eighty percent of the land is still covered in forest, and there are still large tracts of wilderness. Bordering with Quebec and New Brunswick along the frontier, the landscape shows all the signs of the turmoil it experienced during the last Ice Age. The furrows and scars of glaciation are today marked by lakes and ponds and ragged inlets. From fertile Aroostook ("the County"),

the Allagash River (designated a "wilderness waterway") leads south to Telos Lake. Its course through an unspoiled swathe of conifer forest may be followed by canoe. To the east, Baxter State Park typifies the wild north of Maine, covering some 200,000 acres of forest between Webster Brook and the noble brow of Mount Katahdin, which rises to 5,267 feet (1,605 m). The area can be reached by driving north from Millinocket (west off Interstate 95). The **Appalachian National Scenic Trail** starts here, following the ridges southward through 14 states to Georgia's Springer Mountain. Some backpackers tackle the whole stretch – it takes about four to five months.

Maine is the easternmost state in the Union, the first to catch the dawn. The **Moosehead National Wildlife Refuge** lies at the very edge of the continent, and a network of other reserves stretches westward, including **Cross Island, Petit Manan, Franklin Island,** and **Rachel Carson,** named after the author of *The Silent Spring,* which on its publication in 1962 did so much to arouse the ecological conscience of the nation. These offer a secure habitat for pelagic birds, waterfowl, eagles, woodcocks, deer, and bears. The **Carlton Pond Waterfowl Production Area** is off U.S. Highway 202 at Troy.

Above: Once the height of modernity, today Mount Washington's cog railway seems almost to have become part of the mountain itself as it puffs its way to the summit and back.

Left: Salt spray on the wind and surging seas characterize the Acadian shore line. One of the most unspoiled parts of the New England coast, Acadia has retained a special charm of its own.

Overleaf: Light floods across the ridges of Vermont's Green Mountains. Hikers stand silhouetted as they look south to the Green Mountain National Forest, which forms a good half of the state's public lands.

In 1604 the French explorer Samuel de Champlain (1567–1635) ran aground on Mount Desert Island, known to the Abnaki Indians as Pemetic. Southern Maine became an area of French and British rivalry during the eighteenth century. This magical region is known as Acadia, and few places in New England can capture the spirit of the North Atlantic so perfectly. The **Acadia National Park** was established in 1919, and its 38,524 acres are divided into three sections. Isle au Haut is the southernmost, reached by passenger ferry from Stonington, south on Maine 15. The largest section covers part of Mount Desert Island either side of Somes Sound, off Maine 3 and 102. Across Frenchman Bay, the Schoodic Peninsula is circled by a one-way loop off Maine 186, between Winter Harbor and Birch Harbor.

The area is best viewed from Cadillac Mountain (1,530 feet; 465 m) on Mount Desert Island. From here one can see the granite mountains, ground into humps by ancient glaciation, the lakes, ponds, dark green strips of forest, and the open waters of the Atlantic Ocean, misty or clear, gray or blue. The waves plow into tumbled slabs of rock with a vengeance. Lighthouses stand sentinel, and herring gulls circle overhead. Beachcombing is fascinating, due to the variety of shells, seaweeds, and flotsam; tidal rockpools reveal worlds within worlds. Offshore, fishermen catch cod, sardine, or lobster.

Visitors come to Acadia to walk the shoreline or hike the inland trails. The park has 120 miles of footpaths. Cycling, riding, camping, birdwatching, fishing, swimming, and boating are among the many park activities, and for motorists there are many fine overlooks and vistas. To find out more about Acadia and its history, call at the visitor center south of Hulls Cove, and pay a visit to the museums at Sieur de Monts Spring and Little Cranberry Island.

From a narrow coastal frontage, the state of New Hampshire opens out into a pastoral landscape with rivers and lakes. The towns are of traditional white clapboard houses, picket fences, warm brick façades, and peaceful, leafy streets. From Lake Winnepesaukee the countryside stretches westward to the Connecticut River and northward to Canada. This gentle idyll is interrupted by terrain of a more rugged nature. The **White Mountain National Forest** takes up a total of 728,623 acres in central New Hampshire, crossed by the **Appalachian National Scenic Trail**. The forest is of birch and sugar maple – stunningly beautiful in its fall livery – giving way to spruce and fir at higher altitudes. The forest's highest point, rising above the Great Gulf Wilderness, is Mount Washington, at 6,288 feet (1,917 m). Although it is scaled by a rack-and-pinion railway and crowned by an observatory, the mountain remains untamed above the treeline. Its summit is notorious for attracting some of the most extreme weather conditions conceivable: winds more powerful than any hurricane, heavy snowfall, and storms made in Valhalla. Hikers and climbers should be on their guard, but not deterred. The White Mountains are an uplifting experience. A succession of rolling heights stretches into the blue distance, from Washington's neighbors in the Presidential group onwards. In the summer you can hike the trails, or drive on the summit road; in the winter you can ski. Campgrounds are readily available, if popular, in the summer; some are open in winter too. Scenic New Hampshire 16 travels northward through the region, and U.S. Highway 302 and Interstate 93 also give access. In the south, New Hampshire 112 slips between Mount Huntington and Mount Osceola. Ranger stations are in Conway, Compton, and Lincoln.

New Hampshire's neighbor across the Connecticut River is Vermont, bordered to the south by Massachusetts, to the east by New York State and Lake Champlain, and to the north by Quebec in Canada. Vermont is a gem of a state, famous all over the world for its display of foliage in the fall. In the nineteenth century, about 70 percent of the state was open farmland, and the rest wooded. Today the balance has gone the other way, and forest management burns out growth in places to ensure the survival of established bird and mammal species. The wooded valleys of the imposing Appalachian ranges are interspersed with pretty villages, and in winter the sparkling mountains attract many thousands of skiing enthusiasts.

The **Green Mountain National Forest** occupies 295,007 acres in the center and south of the state, east of U.S. Highway 7. The northern section is bounded by U.S. Highway 4, Vermont 116 and 100, and crossed by Vermont 125 and 73. The forest surrounds the Bristol Cliff and Breadloaf wildernesses, and the Long Trail runs from north to south across the latter. Another trail in this section commemorates Robert Frost (1874–1963), New England's most famous poet. The southern section, west of Manchester, is crossed by Vermont 8, 9, 11, 30, and 100. It includes the **White Rocks National Recreation Area** and the wildernesses of Big Banks, Peru Peak, Lye Brook, and George D. Aiken. The **Appalachian National Scenic Trail** runs along the hills; on this and the coinciding Long Trail, shelters are placed at regular intervals for long-distance hikers. Here are many famous winter sports areas. The forest has nine developed campgrounds and many picnic sites for those who wish to enjoy a leisurely excursion through this beautiful neck of the backwoods.

Both the White Mountain and Green Mountain national forests form a vital reservoir of wildlife in the Northeast, a haven for deer, bears, and birdlife. Two national wildlife refuges in the region also help sustain the

The snowy summit of Mount Washington rises from the woodlands of the White Mountain National Forest. Some 1,425 miles of trail lead hikers through the forest and over the mountains of New Hampshire.

balance of nature in the face of encroaching urbanization. The New Hampshire Appalachians' **Wapack Reserve** and Vermont's **Missiquoi Reserve** (a wetlands habitat on Lake Champlain) are of interest to ornithologists. In Massachusetts, too, nature reserves are conserving the natural environment close to urban areas: **Great Meadows**, near Boston; **Oxbow**, on the Nashua; **Parker River** on the coast. The **Nantucket National Wildlife Refuge** is on the old whalers' island, the haunt of many a Captain Ahab in the last century. To the south, fresh and saltwater habitats combine to attract waterfowl and seabirds to **Monomoy National Wildlife Refuge**.

Massachusetts is an elegant and historic state. Small, civilized towns are its hallmark, with many buildings recalling the early days of European settlement, as at Salem and Plymouth. The state has 598,900 acres of agricultural land. Sixty-eight percent of the countryside is forested, producing white ash, northern red oak, sugar maple, white pine, and hemlock.

North of Nantucket Sound, Cape Cod symbolizes the history of this maritime state, from the *Mayflower* to Marconi, who set up his Wireless Station here in 1901. The Cape is partly a glacial moraine dating from the last Ice Age. Erosion by human exploitation as well as by natural forces led to the creation of the **Cape Cod National Seashore**, which enabled 44,596 acres of this unique environment to be cared for in an appropriate manner. The seaside atmosphere and fine old buildings of the Cape bring many tourists to the area in the summer, in order to surf, swim, ride horses, or cycle. Exploring the beaches and watching the seabirds and ships, one feels liberated by the space of the open Atlantic: Between here

A lighthouse stands sentinel over the Massachusetts coast at Cape Cod. This peninsula of eroding beaches and shifting dunes has long been a favorite with tourists. In 1961 a section of Cape Cod between Chatham and Provincetown was declared a national seashore.

Mists roll in from the Atlantic, shrouding the historical skyline of Cape Cod. This long headland played an important role in America's colonial past, and still has an aura of bygone days.

and the rocky shores of western Europe is nothing but the green ocean swell. U.S. Highway 6 curves around Cape Cod Bay and then turns north to the national seashore area. The Salt Pond Visitor Center is in the south, an area which includes Red Maple Swamp, Fort Hill, Salt Pond Bay, and Naunset Marsh. Champlain's 1605 charts show the latter as an open bay, surrounded by Indian settlements. Continuing northward, U.S. 6 skirts the seashore, with spurs leading off to the beach. Near the Marconi site, explore the Atlantic White Cedar Swamp Trail. West of Wellfleet, a sandy trail crosses Great Island. The trees here were felled for the whaling fleet, and in 1831 emergent sandbanks linked the deforested island to the Cape. Passing North Truro and the Head of the Meadow, the road skirts Pilgrim's Lake. Seaward are the dunes; to the west and south, Provincetown Harbor. An extension road leads to the Province Lands Visitor Center, Race Point, and the Beech Forest Trail. Both visitor centers are closed in winter, when information is available from Race Point Ranger Station. Camping is available at the Nickerson State Park, East Brewster, but is not allowed within the national seashore area.

Rhode Island is the thirteenth and smallest state of the Union, with an

Ospreys may still be seen on the Rhode Island coast at the national wildlife refuges of Ninigret and Trustom Pond. These magnificent predators use their powerful talons to catch fish.

area of only 1,214 square miles. It surrounds the long inlet of Narragansett Bay and the Sakonnet River, and the state capital of Providence. The coastline is preserved at a number of national wildlife refuges. **Sachuest Point** (221 acres) is on Aquidneck Island at Middletown, east of Newport. Grasslands and saltmarsh border the dunes of the beaches, providing a stopover for migratory black duck and other wildfowl, such as eider, old squaw, and scoter. Waders frequent the littoral zone; the marshes harbor snapping turtles, bitterns, and herons, while the grassy areas support foxes, rodents, and short-eared owls. To the west, the **Ninigret National Wildlife Refuge** (404 acres) contains similar habitats, another stopover on the long north-south migratory route known as the Atlantic Flyway. Common terns breed here, and large raptors such as bald eagles and ospreys are on the species list. Outdoor pursuits in the refuge include hiking, photography, and, in winter, cross-country skiing. **Trustom Pond National Wildlife Refuge** (579 acres), a popular recreational area, is a breeding site for piping plovers and least terns. **Block Island**, reached by toll ferry from Newport, and from New London, Connecticut, is another important nesting site and wildfowl area. Its national wildlife refuge of 29 acres is on the north coast of the island. In the southwest are the impressive Mohegan Bluffs, a 5-mile wall of clay buffeted by the Atlantic. In summer Block Island's beaches and fishing attract many tourists.

To the west, the full force of the ocean is shielded by Long Island's twin headlands, Montauk and Orient Points. The coast of Connecticut, rising from Long Island Sound, is the haunt of yachting enthusiasts. The hinterland, bisected by the Connecticut River, includes pleasant countryside as well as large urban areas. The state has about half a million acres of farmland and is famed for its spring blossoms and fall colors. Yale University has been at New Haven since the early eighteenth century, and historic towns and coastal resorts attract tourists. A small corner of the coastline at **Salt Meadows** has been set aside for other colonizers of the coast – songbirds, waterfowl, and wading birds. The natural habitat is woodland and coastal marshes. New York national wildlife refuges in the Long Island Sound region include **Morton, Target Rock**, and **Oyster Bay.**

New York is known universally for its city, the great sprawl of suburbs, apartment blocks, office buildings, shops, and streets that stretches from Long Island to New Jersey, culminating in the thrilling, infuriating, throbbing streets of Manhattan. To many of the city's 9 million inhabitants, the world ends at Coney Island. However, upstate New York could be no greater contrast to the bustle of the "Big Apple." The state has 10 million acres of farmland and orchards, as well as peaceful hills, rivers, and lakes. The Hudson River Valley, the Catskills, and the Adirondacks offer often beautiful scenery in a historic setting. The **Adirondack Park** is a huge area of lakes and wooded crests; over 500 miles of hiking trails cross its 6 million acres. Beyond, the Canadian

Mohegan Bluffs, tawny-colored cliffs which rise 180 feet (55 m) above the waves of the Atlantic Ocean, on Block Island, R.I. Block Island is a popular summer resort for tourists, famed for its offshore fishing.

border follows the St. Lawrence, Lake Ontario, the Niagara, and Lake Erie.

In all the eastern states, no natural spectacle arouses such interest as **Niagara Falls**. It was always so. Five allied Indian tribes used to occupy the New York region – the Mohawk, Oneida, Cayuga, Onondaga, and Seneca. Together they formed the Iroquoian confederacy. To these Indians, the Falls had long been famed in legend and folklore. It was the Seneca who guarded the western approaches to Iroquois territory, around Niagara. In 1678 a French priest, Père Louis Hennepin, reached their lands, and was dumbfounded by the Falls. His traveler's tales were to spread around Europe like wildfire. The French built a fort here, and the area was bitterly fought over between British and French, and then between Americans and British. The nineteenth century was the era of engineering marvels: The Erie Canal was opened in 1825 and the Roebling Suspension Bridge 30 years later. It was also the age of industrialization, and the flow became exploited for hydraulic and then hydroelectric power. Above all, this was the age of gimcrack showmanship and derring-do. In 1829 Sam Patch threw himself into the torrent, and in 1859–60 French tightrope artist "Charles Blondin" (Jean-François Gravelet, 1824–97) performed balancing acts across the chasm. The doughty Captain Matthew Webb (1848–83), the first person to swim the English Channel, drowned in his attempt to swim the Niagara rapids. And so the thundering Niagara Falls became associated with cheap stunts, industrial enterprises, tourist attractions, and honeymoon hotels.

And yet the Falls themselves were not demeaned, rather the people who would set their egos against the implacable power of nature. Visiting Niagara Falls today is still an experience that leaves one speechless. The Niagara – strictly a strait between Erie and Ontario rather than a river –

Spray forms a hazy cloud above the Horseshoe Falls at Niagara, on the border between New York State and Canada. This relentless flow of water is exploited for hydroelectric power. The Niagara Falls were the nation's earliest tourist attraction, coming under state care in 1885. Today, visitors from all over the world are still thrilled by the spectacle.

powers itself over precipitous cliffs, to fall in wide curtains of white water, rainbows forming in the fine spray. The American Falls drop 184 feet (56 m) over a section of rock 1,060 feet (320 m) wide. The Horseshoe Falls, carrying the lion's share of the flood, drop 176 feet (54 m) over a length of 2,200 feet (675 m). The natural flow of the Niagara is 202,000 cubic feet per second (5,720 cubic meters per second), although hydroelectric requirements divert part of the flow. The statistics are impressive, although other falls in the United States can better them. It is, however, the sheer massiveness and power which moves one at Niagara. At night the Falls are illuminated, the lights powered by their own turbines.

Visitors can view the Falls in various ways. They can take a helicopter trip, or don waterproofs and take a boat (the famous *Maid of the Mists*) to the very edge of the cascade. An observation tower at Prospect Point offers views of the American Falls. Another vantage point is Goat Island, which lies between the American Falls and Horseshoe Falls. At the Niagara Power Project Visitor Center one can learn how the waters are harnessed for their energy, and look down on the Niagara and its gorge. Old Fort Niagara reminds one of the colonial period, the days of Redcoats, Iroquois, and French explorers. The town of Niagara Falls is to the north of Buffalo off Interstate 80.

Due west of Niagara Falls, the **Iroquois National Wildlife Refuge** (10,818 acres) contains pools and woods which attract geese and swans migrating from the tundra regions of the north. Beavers dam the lakes, and whitetailed deer break cover. West of the Iroquois one enters the Finger Lakes region of New York State. On the northern end of Cayuga Lake is the **Montezuma National Wildlife Refuge** (6,432 acres). Seneca Falls is 2 miles to the south, on U.S. Highway 20. The surrounding wetland, as in many parts of the nation, was severely depleted by drainage during the early years of this century. The refuge was set up in 1937 in order to make amends for this unwitting vandalism. Huge flocks of Canada geese and ducks congregate here in the spring and fall, thanks to the restitution of the natural environment. A program aimed at restoring the bald eagle to New York, a state from which it had virtually disappeared, has met with some success. The official list records 314 bird species as having been observed at the refuge. Observation towers, a nature trail, and a drive are available for public use, and fishing is permitted. Teachers of environmental studies use the refuge as a practical demonstration of conservation methods.

Long Island is a popular weekend retreat from the rigors of metropolitan life, with pleasant countryside, small towns of period charm, and ocean beaches. Its southern coast is guarded by a narrow 32-mile-long barrier of sand, saltmarsh, and scrub, with clusters of pine and hardwood. Landward, the barrier encloses Great South Bay, Moriches Bay, and Shinnecock Bay. **Fire Island National Seashore** occupies 19,579 acres west of Robert Moses State Park. There are private holiday homes here, but most of the long expanse of beach is unspoiled, despite being less than a couple of hours away from New York City. There are no roads on Fire Island except at the access points via tollbridge from Bayshore or Shirley. Ferries run from Bayshore, Sayville, and Patchogue. You may catch a glimpse of a fox on Fire Island, and deer may also be seen. Waterfowl and herons are attracted to the marshes, and seabirds squabble offshore. In the west, Sailor's Haven has a visitor center and offers swimming, boating, and picnicking, as well as a nature trail; the same facilities attract visitors to Watch Hill, in the center of the island, which is reached by boat and ferry. Here one can reserve camping sites in summer months. Smith Point West, accessible from Shirley, also has a visitor center. Clams are much sought after, and anglers fish the surf for bluefish, kingfish, and striped bass. Others prefer to laze on the beach, and watch the changing patterns of sea and sky.

The state of New Jersey is bounded to the northeast by a dense conurbation along the Hudson, and to the east by its ocean coast and the

Overleaf: A snowfall complements the unique beauty of the Niagara Falls. Although the region is thoroughly urbanized, the Falls retain a primitive magic. Between Lake Erie and Lake Ontario, the waters of the Niagara drop 326 feet (99 m): More than half the descent is in this single plunge over bluffs of limestone and shale.

31

An adult beaver with a youngster just seven days old. Beavers are among the 33 mammal species recorded in the wetlands of the Iroquois National Wildlife Refuge in upstate New York. Beavers are today common in the region, despite a history of persecution by fur trappers.

barrier outposts of Island Beach and Long Beach Island. South of Absecon Inlet is the popular seaside resort of Atlantic City, with its casinos, boardwalks, and vacationing hordes. And that, one might think, is that. But that would be to forget the lakes and the hills of the Kittatinny Ridge in the northeast of the state, the **Appalachian National Scenic Trail**, the ski slopes of Vernon Valley, the forests of Wawayanda and Worthington; it would be to ignore the broad, sinuous passage of the historic Delaware, separating the state from Pennsylvania in the west. It would be to forget that, despite urbanization, this is the "Garden State,"

After the claustrophobic bustle of New York City, Fire Island offers its summer residents peaceful open spaces and sea breezes. This long barrier to the south of Long Island consists largely of dunes and sparse vegetation.

Sand and sea: Fire Island, N.Y., was established as a national seashore in 1964. Long summer days are spent on the beach, swimming, or walking alongside the bracing Atlantic, or sea angling.

The tangled thickets of New Jersey's Great Swamp provide a perfect habitat for waterfowl and other birds. In recognition of this, over 675,000 acres of this densely forested marshland have been preserved as a national wildlife refuge.

with over a million acres of farmland. Of course, since the first settlers sailed up the Delaware, the fertile land on the east bank has changed beyond all recognition – yet it still surprises. The state is almost entirely surrounded by water, fresh or salt, and wetland areas remain a boon for bird life. Barnegat, west of Island Beach, is an area of swamps, creeks, and woods. The **Barnegat National Wildlife Refuge** covers 10,200 acres east of U.S. Highway 9 and the Garden State Parkway, and attracts migratory waterfowl, herons, and egrets. Inland to the north, the **Great Swamp National Wildlife Refuge** is dangerously near to New York

Pause for reflection: New Jersey's Great Swamp presents an image of tranquility in the heart of the urban northeast. Conservationists have to fight hard to preserve the few rural areas which have managed to escape the spread of the big cities.

City, but has miraculously escaped drainage and development. Here, virgin woodland roots in ferny swamps adjacent to higher ground. Mink and foxes live in the refuge; booming bitterns and the injury-feigning killdeer as well as wood ducks make this a mecca for birdwatchers from the big city.

Across the Delaware Bay, the second smallest state of the Union looks out across the Atlantic. Settled in 1638, this state played an important part in the early history of the United States, and many historic buildings may still be seen. Over half a million acres of Delaware is farmland, but this is primarily an industrial region. Waterfowl winging their way up the Atlantic Flyway track down two large wetland sites on the Delaware coast. **Bombay Hook National Wildlife Refuge** extends over 15,099 acres northeast of Dover. To the south, the **Prime Hook Refuge** is 8,926 acres.

The importance of such areas is brought sharply into focus at the **Tinicum National Environment Center** in neighboring Pennsylvania. The 1,200-acre site forms the very last stretch of tidal marsh in the state, amid encroaching urban development. This oasis supports indigenous fauna. Pennsylvania is a fascinating state, stretching from Lake Erie to the Atlantic, from the Ohio River to the Delaware River, and crossed by the Susquehanna. The former territory of the Algonquian Delaware Indians is now industrialized in many areas, and Philadelphia, Penn's "City of Brotherly Love," is now a great metropolis, matched in the west by Pittsburgh, the iron and steel giant. For all its industrial muscle, Pennsylvania has retained a large amount of agricultural land – over 8 million acres – and broad patches of deciduous forest. It also has the scenery of the Alleghenies and the Appalachian National Scenic Trail, which winds south from the Pocono Mountains on its long journey southward.

The **Delaware Water Gap National Recreation Area** is the name

Idyllic landscapes have attracted many an artist to the locality of the Delaware Water Gap over the years. Twenty years ago this was declared a national recreation area, and today many visitors come to explore the area by boat or to hike the trails.

Cloud lies low over the Delaware Water Gap. Here the Delaware River winds its way between Pennsylvania's Pocono Plateau and New Jersey's Kittatinny Mountains, below cliffs 1,000 feet (305 m) high. Laurel and hemlock rise from the ridges.

Overleaf: Timber stands high above the Cornplanter Bridge on the Allegheny Reservoir. Extending northward to cross the New York line, the reservoir is popular with weekend campers and boating enthusiasts. The Allegheny National Forest stretches southward, blanketing the rolling hills of Pennsylvania. Seneca Indians originally inhabited this forest, most of which was felled by early settlers and by the tanning industry. Amends were made in 1923, when President Coolidge created a national forest in the area. Small sections of the original forest have survived; the rest has been planted.

38

now given to the latter beauty spot. This is a 35-mile-long pass between New Jersey's Kittatinny Mountains and the Pocono Plateau. In the Lenape Indian tongue *pocono* or *poco-hanne* meant the "stream between the mountains;" *kittatinny* meant "endless hills." The Delaware River sweeps through this breach in the ancient fold mountains, cutting through high cliffs on either side. Hardwood forest greens the hills, which shelter raccoons, squirrels, foxes, whitetailed deer, even the occasional black bear or timber rattlesnake. High above, keen-eyed hawks scan the hills. In the past, the gap attracted visitors, especially artists in search of a picturesque landscape. Many more visitors arrive today: The scenery is as delightful as ever, and this is ideal touring country. However, the emphasis has changed a little. One former vacation resort has now become the Pocono Environmental Education Center, a base for field studies where students can study the ecology of the region. Rock climbing is a popular activity around the Water Gap, as is boating and canoeing. Access to the water is near Bushkill, at Poxono, Smithfield Beach, and Kittatinny. For hikers, fine trails have been blazed across the woods and hills. There are 25 miles of the Appalachian Trail, and excellent views of the Water Gap are to be obtained from the Mount Tammany and Mount Minsi trails. Naturalists should follow the Slate Quarry and the Thunder Mountain trails (the latter winds around a beaver pond). Near Dingman's Ferry a trail leads to Dingman's Falls and Silver Thread Falls, an idyll made perfect when the rhododendrons are in bloom. Fishing is popular in the Delaware and the lakes and streams of the forest. Trout, shad, bluegill, and walleye number among the catch. In winter, ice-fishing is possible, together with ice-skating and ski-touring. The Water Gap is beautiful under snow, with the crowds of the summer far away. Since the Delaware Water Gap was established as a national recreation area in 1965, the history of the area has not been overlooked. The settlement of Millbrook has been refurbished as typical of a rural town of the late nineteenth century; at the height of the season there are tours around the old school, the church, and the stores. The artistic traditions of the region have not been neglected either, and arts and crafts are produced at the village of Peter's Valley. Delaware Water Gap is located off Interstate 80 and stretches north along both banks of the Delaware to below Port Jervis on Interstate 84. There are no campgrounds or other accommodation facilities within the national recreation area, but they are available in the vicinity.

In the northwest of Pennsylvania the **Allegheny National Forest** covers 510,500 acres, a patchwork of hardwoods covering the undulating hills south of New York State and east of Lake Erie. Green in spring and russet in fall, the scenery is viewed from U.S. Highway 6, Pennsylvania 66, 321, 666, and 948, which all pass through the area. Interstate 80, the main route westward, lies to the south. The story of this forest is one of survival against all odds. Ruthlessly cleared in the last century, and decimated by fires, the forest growth has now crept back over the exhausted land, thanks to the dogged conservation work of the National Forest Service. Today the ridges are felled commercially but with responsibility. At the same time they offer a habitat to deer and bear, and enable city-dwellers to breathe some fresh air into their lungs. Outdoor pursuits include fishing, hiking, horse riding, and camping. The Allegheny River penetrates the forest on its 325-mile journey from New York State to the Ohio River at Pittsburgh. Dammed at Kinzua, the long shores of the reservoir form a ragged rent across the state line. To the west of the forest, the **Erie National Wildlife Refuge** maintains 7,994 acres of lakeland with an eye to the twice yearly migration of waterfowl.

Some 69 square miles of territory along the Potomac River occupies land ceded to the nation by the state of Maryland. Established by Acts of Congress in 1790–1, the District of Columbia is the site of Washington, the federal capital. Its monuments and historic buildings are most impressive, and the corridors of green give the city a feeling of spaciousness rare in other world capitals. "D.C." is of course entirely urbanized, but passing mention should be made of the **Theodore Roosevelt Memorial Island**. Approached from a footbridge on the Virginia shore, this 88-acre island in the Potomac, complete with nature trails, is intended as a monument to the 26th president's achievements as a conservationist. Roosevelt (1858–1919) was in many ways a man of contradictions. Like many of his era, he was an enthusiastic hunter, but he was also a keen zoologist. Born in New York, he fell in love with the wilderness of the North Dakota badlands. A successful Washington politician, he was happiest when ranching or exploring the wilds of Africa. If it hadn't been for Teddy Roosevelt and others like him, however, this book would probably not have been written, for more than any other politician he threw his weight behind the creation of national parks, and supported the establishment of national forests in the teeth of commercial opposition. In short, he ensured the survival of America's natural heritage. A monument to him stands on the island.

The state of Maryland is a cartographer's nightmare, the border

A green backwater in the midst of the District of Columbia commemorates Theodore Roosevelt. The former U.S. President's Memorial Island in the Potomac is a monument to his pioneering work in defence of the American landscape. Roosevelt set aside vast tracts of land as national parks and forests, and created the first national wildlife refuge.

zigzagging around the divide of Chesapeake Bay and meandering with the course of the Potomac. The region was surveyed in the years 1763–7 by Charles Mason and Jeremiah Dixon, and became famous as the line between the "slave" states and the free North. The Appalachians cross the western part of Maryland, rising to 3,360 feet (1,024 m) at Backbone Mountain in the southeastern corner of the state. Parts of Maryland are industrial, with large-scale urban development around Baltimore. Suburbs stretch north from Washington D.C. Many of the state's historic buildings are set in farmland; 43 percent of the state remains agricultural.

Like so much of the eastern seaboard, Maryland's Atlantic coast is fringed by a long, sandy island barrier. The **Assateague Island National Seashore** (51,200 acres) is 37 miles long and stretches from Ocean City to Chincoteague, Virginia, east of U.S. Highway 113. Between these two poles, the narrow, roadless spit of sand and saltmarsh sustains scrub and woodland, and a varied wildlife. Its most famous inhabitants are the Chincoteague ponies, sturdy creatures which run wild and free. The

Peaceful moorings on Assateague Island. This national seashore stretches southward into Virginia, and encloses coastal wetlands frequented by migrating waterfowl.

45

The summer visitors have gone, and gale-force winds whip Atlantic breakers to a fury on Assateague Island National Seashore, during winter storms.

Chincoteague National Wildlife Refuge occupies 12 miles of the strip, and is visited by waterfowl on their long coastal haul. The national seashore offers primitive camping, angling from the beach, canoeing, and hiking; away from the access roads it is empty and often exhilarating, a chance to be alone with the wind and the sea.

On the western side of the peninsula, another two national wildlife refuges cater for waterfowl. **Blackwater National Wildlife Refuge** (14,263 acres) lies off Maryland 335 south of Cambridge; **Eastern Neck** is an island of 2,286 acres on the Chester River in northern Chesapeake Bay. Both reserves have a woodland and marsh habitat and protect rare fox squirrels.

The federal land of **Greenbelt Park** covers 1,167 acres northeast of Washington D.C. The park consists of gentle woodland and short trails. These loop through stands of pine and beautiful azaleas. Here you can escape from the city grime for a taste of the countryside and enjoy horse riding, cycling, walking, or camping. A rather longer journey from the federal capital will take you to **Catoctin Mountain Park**, 65 miles into the Appalachian ridges of the north. Approach via Maryland 77 off U.S. Highway 15; the park is adjacent to Maryland's Cunningham State Park. The rolling forest landscape above the Monocacy Valley is crossed by clear streams and can be explored by trails, bridle paths, and a scenic drive. Summer camping is available at Owen's Creek, and trout fishing is popular. The park area's natural beauty today is the result of three decades of reclamation work, for this area was in the past stripped of its timber and over-farmed.

West Virginia became a state in its own right in 1863: It broke away from Virginia when the latter voted to secede from the Union and side with the Confederates. Its eastern border is formed by the Shenandoah Mountains and the broad sweep of the Alleghenies: Spruce Knob is the state's highest point, at 4,860 feet (1,480 m). The state's western border follows the Ohio River. Underground, over half the state has quality coal. On the surface, small farms account for about 4 million acres of West Virginia, and three-fourths of the state is wooded. These facts add up to a land of white water and rolling mountains, of covered bridges and old villages tucked away in the valleys, of industrial development and a hardy, independent people.

The east of the state is one of the most scenic parts of the nation. Virginia's George Washington and Jefferson national forests overlap the state line in the east, and the huge **Monongahela National Forest** (842,869 acres) follows the rounded, humpback Appalachians, former pioneer country. The woods here are thickets of broadleaves and conifers, brimming with rivers and waterfalls, and undermined by caverns. Whitetailed deer pick their way over the dappled floor of the forest, and black bears root for berries. Like much of the region, the Monongahela area was worked out at an early date, and only carefully managed forestry has restored it to its rightful state. The Monongahela is crossed by U.S. Highways 33, 250, and 220, and by scenic routes such as West Virginia 28 and 39. The Potomac River rises in Monongahela, and the north fork of its south branch poses a real challenge to white-water enthusiasts. The **Seneca Rocks** region is a national recreation area, and the forest is enjoyed for its canoeing, climbing, trout fishing, winter skiing, and summer camping expeditions. Hiking trails lead to many a dramatic overlook, and the forest has three wilderness areas. One of Monongahela's most unusual sections is the tract of bog and open moorland known as the Dolly Sods area. Plants grow here that are more suited to the Canadian tundra than West Virginia. In early spring, however, blooming rhododendrons bring a touch of color to the dour landscape.

In 1978 the **New River Gorge** was formally recognized as a national river. It clearly deserved the honor, as – ironically in view of its name – it lays claim to being the oldest river in the United States. A 50-mile stretch of the river was set aside between Hinton, on West Virginia 3, and Fayetteville, on U.S. Highway 21. The New River races over some of the

Overleaf: Sunset mellows the hills in West Virginia's New River region, recalling the peaceful landscape settled by the backwoodsmen before the Civil War. Despite subsequent industrial development, the south of the state still affords marvelous scenery.

Meadowland and broadleaved forest rising to Catoctin Mountain Park, Maryland. This peaceable backcountry provides a welcome change for inhabitants of Washington D.C.: a chance to stroll in the woods and breathe fresh air.

The Monongahela National Forest has its headquarters at Elkins, West Virginia. The original forest was one of the finest in the eastern states, comprising oak, chestnut, white pine, hemlock, yellow poplar, and black cherry. After extensive deforestation and settlement, the valleys are now green once again. Typical trees of the northern forest region now include sugar maple, beech, yellow birch, hemlock, red spruce, and balsam fir. The central region includes oaks, hickory, sycamore, sassafras, and original pine.

A whitetailed deer grows its antlers. West Virginia's Monongahela National Forest is home to many wild animals and birds.

meanest rapids in the eastern states, plunging through a precipitous gorge. The park area covers 62,624 acres. The visitor center at the southern end is Canyon Rim; the northern visitor center is at Hinton. It is a sobering thought that the churning water is following a course 100 million years old.

The region around New River was a booming area of coal production in the last century. Today it is a fascinating part of the state to explore, with many natural spectacles and historical sites protected in state parks and forests. One can hike or cycle the 75-mile Greenbrier River Trail from North Caldwell to Cass. West of Interstate 77, visit Pineville to inspect its extraordinary Castle Rock, or visit Pinnacle Rock, a towering pillar of sandstone near Bluefield (off U.S. Highway 52). At Organ Cave, south off U.S. Highway 219, below Interstate 64, a walkway takes you through an extravaganza of limestone formations. One series, when struck, gives out musical notes. During the Civil War, saltpeter (potassium nitrate) for gunpowder was extracted here, under the orders of Robert E. Lee, the Confederate general. Mining gear from the period survives to this day, a poignant reminder of the great conflict that tore the nation apart.

The South

Alabama, Arkansas, Florida, Georgia, Kentucky, North Carolina, South Carolina, Louisiana, Mississippi, Tennessee, Virginia

Florida is the key to the southeastern states. Ponce de Léon's *Pasque de Flores* is a 58,664-square-mile peninsula thrusting southward to the Caribbean Sea. Its day dawns over the Atlantic and ends as the sun sinks into the Gulf of Mexico. To the west, the humid Gulf coast extends in an elongated arc, backed by a lush, fertile plain. This is puddled by swamps and bayous and divided by great confluences and estuaries: the Red River, the Mississippi, the Pearl, the Alabama, the Chattahoochee. The Gulf states are Alabama, Mississippi, and Louisiana. To the northeast are the southern representatives of the Atlantic seaboard: Georgia, South and North Carolina, and Virginia, whose coasts are fringed by barrier islands much of the way to Chesapeake Bay. This, too, is a land of swamps, reservoirs, lakes, and rivers such as the Savannah and Santee. The coastal strip drains the uplands of the interior, which is dominated by the constituent ranges of the Appalachian Chain, such as the Great Smoky Mountains. To the west, the Cumberland Plateau stretches from northern Alabama through eastern Tennessee to Kentucky. West of the Nashville Basin and the valleys of the Tennessee and Mississippi rivers, the state of Arkansas has further highlands: the southern part of the Ozark Plateaux, above the Boston and Ouachita mountains.

The South has many different faces: wooded ridges and hazy blue hills; red dirt roads and green fields; bayous, murky swamps, and trees festooned with mosses; the sullen Mississippi, livid under an electric storm on a summer's afternoon; blazing sunshine and white light; fragrant blossoms; coral reefs and blue seas. The region has a particular enchantment and sense of its own identity. Here, one feels, is a land of history and tradition.

The Southeast was once the home of Indian nations, including the Creek, Choctaw, Chickasaw, Seminoles, and Cherokees, evicted to Oklahoma in the 1830s. Europeans discovered the Gulf coast at an early date. The Spanish explorer Juan Ponce de León landed in Florida in March 1512, and Fernando de Soto (*c.* 1496–1542) explored the Alabama and Mississippi rivers, and probably reached Tennessee. The French explorers Louis Jolliet and Louis Marquette traveled southward down the Mississippi into Arkansas, and the Louisiana region came to be ruled by both France and Spain. A treaty with France secured the South for the nation by the Louisiana Purchase of 1803. On the Atlantic, Virginia was named after English Queen Elizabeth I, the "Virgin Queen;" Jamestown was founded in 1607. The Carolinas and Georgia also saw English colonization, and the backwoods of Tennessee and Kentucky were opened up by pioneers such as Daniel Boone (1735–1820). The southern plantations were important producers of tobacco and cotton. Slave labor was used extensively, and the workforce, of African origin, experienced appalling living conditions. After independence, the issue of slavery tore apart the new nation, and the Civil War of 1861–65 ended with the South devastated and traumatized.

The scars remain even today. Nevertheless, the twentieth century has seen industrialization, new agricultural methods, the development of commerce, and the enforcement of civil rights for the South's black citizens. The South has changed. But its way of life is still leisurely and measured, and much of its scenery remains unspoiled.

Virginia is a state typical of the central Atlantic coast, with urban areas around Norfolk, Richmond, and Roanoke. North of the pleasant sandy shores of Virginia Beach, the coastal plain below the Potomac is indented with the long estuaries of the James, York, and Rapahannock rivers, which drain into Chesapeake Bay under the lee of Cape Charles. The state's western border is formed by the Appalachians. Mount Rogers, in the southwestern corner of the state, is the highest point, rising to 5,719 feet (1,743 m). The difference in altitude between here and the coast is significant and as a result the difference in temperature is considerable.

Some of the finest scenery in the "Old Dominion" surrounds the famous Shenandoah River and the rolling wooded crests of the Blue Ridge and Allegheny mountains. The **Shenandoah National Park** (194,801 acres), founded in 1935, runs southward with the Blue Ridge overlooking the river valley and distant ridges to the west, and the Piedmont Plateau to the east. A scenic highway, the **Skyline Drive**, runs the length of the park, offering magnificent treetop vistas. These ancient mountains became the home of hardy settlers. Their broadleaved forests suffered at the hands of commercial timber interests. The establishment of the national park has allowed the land to recover, and today persimmon, sassafras, oak, and hickory blanket the ridges. In fall the russets and yellows of the leaves present an unforgettable display. Deer browse the range, and squirrels scamper from branch to branch; trout swim the streams. Some 500 miles of hiking and riding trails are to be found in the park, including 95 miles of the **Appalachian National Scenic Trail**, which traverses the Shenandoah en route south from New England. **Skyline Drive** is accessible from Waynesboro or Front Royal, or via U.S. Highways 33 and 211, east of Interstate 81. Camping is available, and further information may be obtained at the visitor centers.

South of Waynesboro, the scenic drive of the toll-free **Blue Ridge Parkway** continues to follow the crests southward all the way to Tennessee. For 469 miles one can pass through the rolling green hills or turn off to explore this historic region. Geological excursions might include Front Royal's Skyline Caverns, the Luray Caverns, or, to the south, the Natural Bridge. Up in the hills one can stop off for a picnic, hike the trails, or fish the streams.

A tributary of the Potomac, the Shenandoah rolls some 200 miles through north Virginia and West Virginia. The Shenandoah National Park is extremely popular with visitors, but turn off the scenic drives to a trailhead and you will discover a quiet world of ferny woods, sparkling mountain streams, and peaceful backwaters. To the Indians, Shenandoah was the "daughter of stars."

The bald eagle, national symbol of the United States, was once very numerous throughout the continent. Today it is only common in Alaska: In the east it has come dangerously near to extinction. Thanks to conservation work, however, this fine raptor may still be seen in Virginia and neighboring states.

The northern section of the Blue Ridge Mountains is surrounded by the 1,054,922 acres of the **George Washington National Forest.** Its Massanutten Visitor Center is open in summer, and ranger stations are at Buena Vista, Covington, Edinburg, Staunton, and Hot Springs. Its southern neighbor is the **Jefferson National Forest** (676,895 acres). Conifers are here mixed with predominantly broadleaved woods, and azaleas and rhododendrons add a touch of exotic color in season. The forest lies on the interface between the northern and southern vegetation zones. The **Appalachian National Scenic Trail** passes through its boundaries, which take in many recreational attractions. Jefferson's headquarters is in Roanoke, with ranger stations in Blacksburg, Wise, Natural Bridge, Marion, New Castle, and Wytheville.

Virginia's varied wildlife is protected in 117,500 acres of national wildlife refuges: **Mason Neck, Chincoteague,** and **Back Bay** on the coast; **Presquile** on the James River; and **Great Dismal Swamp** on the southern border. It may come as surprise to learn that within the gentle Virginia countryside there are still black bears, bald eagles, pileated woodpeckers, sika deer, and feral ponies. The **Prince William Forest Park,** 18,571 acres in the northeast of the state, is little more than a stone's throw from Washington D.C. It harbors whitetailed deer and offers city-dwellers weekend hiking through dense mixed woodland.

The Virginia-Kentucky border country is ruggedly beautiful. Here is Big Black Mountain, the highest point in Kentucky, which rises to a

Cascading water: Whiteoak Canyon may be visited from Mile 42.6 of the famous Skyline Drive. A trail leads to six waterfalls and winds through stands of hemlock. The many streams which lace Shenandoah National Park are home to brook trout and a variety of insects and amphibians.

Branches rimy with frost and snow: Shenandoah National Park in early spring. Once scarred by clearance and settlement, the slopes now support a sturdy growth of trees. Declining mammal species such as the eastern black bear also made a comeback once the park was established.

The surreal underworld of the Mammoth Cave complex lies far beneath the hardwood forests of Kentucky. Here the water table has eaten away the soft substratum of limestone, before subsiding. Exploring the passages is a memorable experience. This is Audubon Avenue on the Historic Tour: Further marvels on the strenuous two-mile walk include Mammoth Dome and Fat Man's Misery.

height of 4,150 feet (1,245 m) above sea level. The **Cumberland Gap National Historical Park** recalls the pioneer days of the eighteenth century and may be explored by scenic hiking trails. Kentucky stretches north and west to the banks of the Ohio, which joins with the Mississippi at Cairo. The Kentucky and Cumberland rivers cross the state, and to the north lies the famous Bluegrass region, its soft hills and paddocks galloped by champion racehorses. The **Daniel Boone National Forest** extends in a long strip along the edge of the Cumberland Plateau. Its 527,971 acres include the magnificent Red River Gorge, lakes, waterfalls, hardwood forest, and limestone caverns.

The world's longest cave system is to be found in Kentucky, undermining ridges along the Green and Nolin rivers. The **Mammoth Cave National Park**, formally established in 1946, is a spelunker's dream, with 301 miles of caves recorded to date. The park may be reached on Kentucky 70 off Interstate 65. The karst region is a maze of caves, sinkholes, underground passageways, and springs. Mammoth Cave's gypsum was mined by pre-Columbian Indians, and in the

Frozen Niagara is the graphic name given to this half-mile tour through the contorted limestone of Mammoth Cave. Six tours take one through some ten miles of the cave system; one tour is specially designed for the physically handicapped.

nineteenth century saltpeter was extracted for gunpowder. Travertine formations create stalactites and stalagmites, joined in places to form enormous pillars. Sheets of calcite hang from the roof. A variety of tours guides you through this Hades, where the temperature is about 54°F (12°C) and the humidity is 87 percent. The park's visitor center will introduce you to the area, where overground pursuits include hiking the woods and nature trails, camping, and cruising the Green River. Permits will be necessary if you wish to camp backcountry.

To the south is Tennessee, prime pioneer territory and the birthplace of Davy Crockett (1786–1836), the backwoodsman and Indian fighter who was elected to Congress and died at the Alamo. Today, cities have grown up around Knoxville in the east, Chattanooga in the south, and Nashville, state capital and center of country music. The state includes large bodies of water around the Tennessee River, with lakes and reservoirs. Woodland and water remain the natural habitat, and the state has five national wildlife refuges: **Reelfoot, Hatchie,** and **Lower Hatchie** in the west; **Tennessee** around Kentucky Lake; and **Cross Creek** in the north.

The **Big South Fork** of the Cumberland River is designated a national river; it flows through a national recreation area noted for its picturesque

The haze of distant horizons. The Great Smoky Mountains take their name from the moisture and hydrocarbons given off by the leaves of plants: These combine with dust to create a milky blue haze over the ridges.

gorges and waterfalls and its historic sites. Its 122,960 acres cross the line into Kentucky's Daniel Boone National Forest, extending as far north as the Yahoo Falls scenic area. The Tennessee sector is approached from Oneida on the Leatherwood Ford Road off U.S. Highway 27. Canoes and rafts tackle the rapids, and fishing for bream, rock, and smallmouth bass is popular. Mining and logging once laid waste much of the Cumberland Plateau. Today the forest has reclaimed the hillsides; green herons still fish the shallows, and peace reigns along the hiking trails and bridle paths. The park headquarters is off the Leatherwood Ford Road in the east.

West of Knoxville to the north of Interstate 40 the **Obed Wild and Scenic River** is surrounded by a 6,451-acre park: This is white water, thrashing over rocks and turbulent pools. The banks of the Obed are of interest to both naturalists and walkers. Tennessee's eastern border is mountainous terrain, its ridges and valleys bristling with the pines and deciduous trees of the **Cherokee National Forest**. Virgin forest runs riot in the splendidly unspoiled **Great Smoky Mountains National Park**, whose 520,004 acres athwart the North Carolina border were set apart in 1926. The hazy hills rise from valley meadows to reach 6,643 feet (2,025 m) at Clingman's Dome. The range includes some of America's most ancient rock formations, and even after eons of weathering they still remain the highest peaks east of the Great Plains. The park has about 800 miles of trails, which lead past abandoned homesteads to the heart of the woods, winding through maple, birch, oak, hickory, pine, and spruce. Wildflowers carpet the floor or forest clearings, and in early summer the purple rhododendrons rise in banks. Bears and deer inhabit the backwoods, and the streams run with trout. Fall is perhaps the best time to hike this section of the **Appalachian National Scenic Trail**, when the trees are ablaze with color. Park headquarters is at Gatlinburg, Tennessee, and there are visitor centers at Sugarlands, Tennessee, and Oconaluftee, North Carolina. There are seven developed campgrounds, of which Cades Cove, Elkmont, and Smokemont are open all year. The park is reached by U.S. Highway 441 southeast of Knoxville. Turn off from Interstate 40 east of Asheville for access from the south.

North Carolina is bounded to the west by the Smokies, and to the east by the Atlantic. From Cape Fear, Onslow Bay sweeps northward to

Lichen-covered boulders and fallen leaves lie strewn across the forest floor in the Great Smoky Mountains National Park. Oak, pine, and beech cover the hills.

The Blue Ridge Parkway runs through Virginia and North Carolina, providing access to some of the most beautiful vistas in the southeast. Trails wind through rolling hills and forests which provide colorful displays of foliage in the fall.

Cape Lookout. The Neuse and Pamlico rivers enter the lagoon of Pamlico Sound, while the Roanoke, Chowan, Perquimans, and Pasquotank drain into Albermarle Sound. In the west of the state, the Great Smoky Mountains National Park is bounded by the beautiful **Nantahala** and **Pisgah National Forests**, over a million acres of woodland incorporating the Joyce Kilmer-Slickrock Wilderness area. Joyce Kilmer (1888–1919) is remembered for the poem "Trees:"

> I think that I shall never see
> A poem lovely as a tree.

On the Piedmont Plateau, the **Uwharrie National Forest** is primarily a commercial enterprise. To the south is the **Pee Dee National Wildlife Refuge**. The coastal region has five similar refuges, with **Mackay Island** in the north; **Pea Island**, **Pungo**, and **Swanquarter** in the middle; and **Cedar Island** in the south. These cater primarily for seabirds and the waterfowl of the Atlantic flyway. The coastal **Croatan National Forest** is another working forest, with stands of loblolly and longleaf pine. The peat soil is a remnant of a great wetland which once extended all the way to the Great Dismal Swamp. Black bears, deer, and wild turkeys inhabit the forest. Hikers can explore the area via the Cedar Point Tideland Trail or the Island Creek Forest Walk.

The full impact of the Atlantic's blue-green swell is preempted by a long string of offshore islands which act as a barrier. These are the Outer Banks, a thin and fragile defense against the ocean. The nation's first national seashore, **Cape Hatteras** was established in 1937. It incorporates 30,319 acres of sandspit and dunes, the graveyard of many a sailing ship. Many broken hulks still protrude from the sand, their timbers bleached by wind, sun, and salt. Trees which grew on the islands of Bodie, Ocracoke, and Hatteras were felled for shipbuilding and ship repair and for building; today the remaining vegetation is chiefly dunegrass with occasional yaupon. Golden, wind-rippled high dunes are a feature of the Outer Banks. In the summer these attract swimmers, surfers, and campers; anglers and deep-sea fishers catch bass, bluefish, marlin, and sailfish. U.S. Highway 158 runs south from Kitty Hawk, where the Wright brothers made their historic flight on December 17 1903. U.S. Highways 64 and 264 link Mann's Harbor with Nags Head, and North Carolina 12 runs the gauntlet of the banks to the south. Ferries cross Hatteras Inlet and run from Cedar Island and Swanquarter.

Since 1966 the undeveloped southern islands of the Outer Banks have

Timber decline in the Pisgah National Forest near Mount Mitchell. Forestry management was pioneered in this region and is still studied today. Parts of this forest are splendid with rhododendron and azalea. The Blue Ridge Parkway provides access to this interesting area.

also been preserved, as the **Cape Lookout National Seashore**. Access is by boat, or by ferry from Harkers Island, Davis, or Atlantic. The black-and-white tower of Cape Lookout Lighthouse overlooks a lonely world of saltmarsh and surf, a beachcomber's paradise. To the west is Core Sound, to the east Core Banks and the open seas of Raleigh Bay, named after Sir Walter Raleigh (1552–1618), the English navigator and colonial entrepreneur.

The state of South Carolina is bounded to the northwest by the **Wild and Scenic Chattooga River**, which tumbles over cascades and rapids, with 50 miles of riverside extending into North Carolina and Georgia. Canoeing the white water is exhilarating, though it should be emphasized that certain sections should only be tackled by the experienced. The border overlaps the southern end of the Blue Ridge, which at Sassafras Mountain reaches 3,548 feet (1,081 m). Rivers spill southward: the Savannah (forming the Georgia line), the Saluda, the Catawba, and the Pee Dee. The central Piedmont Plateau descends to a swampy coastal plain and the gentle arc of Long Bay. Over 900 square miles of the state is taken up by inland water such as Lake Moultrie and Lake Marion, above the Santee Dam.

The **Sumter National Forest** (357,424 acres) takes its name from Thomas Sumter (1734–1832), the American general who fought the British in South Carolina during the War of Independence. The western unit of the forest is the Andrew Pickens; its pines and hardwoods rise on the mountain slopes of the Blue Ridge. South Carolina 28 and 107 (off U.S. Highway 123) lead to the heart of the backwoods. The southern unit is Long Cane, named for the switch cane which grows here on the Georgia line. Here, in former Cherokee lands, the Savannah River is now damned to create the Clark Hill Reservoir. Explore the region from McCormick on U.S. Highway 221. In the northeast, the Enoree Unit is pine plantation, near Newberry on Interstate 26.

The **Francis Marion National Forest** (249,401 acres) is named for another hero of the fight against the British. Brigadier-general Francis Marion (1732–95), of Huguenot descent, was a wily irregular; to the British under General Banastre Tarleton he was the "old swamp fox." A

Cape Hatteras lighthouse overlooks a broad expanse of sand and wild ocean on the Outer Banks. The tallest lighthouse in the U.S.A., it was constructed in 1870. Together with the lights on Bodie (1872) and Ocracoke (1823), it has saved the lives of many sailors: The banks have long been notorious for shifting shallows and sudden storms.

An Ocracoke fisherman checks his tackle. The island, part of Cape Hatteras National Seashore, may be reached by ferry from Swanquarter and Cedar Island, North Carolina. A road traverses the island from Ocracoke Village, linking up with the free ferry service to Hatteras Island. The local people have a long tradition of seafaring and marine rescue.

visit to this forest on the coastal plain makes one sympathize with Tarleton. Here was a tangle of live oak, dogwood, loblolly pine, cypress, gum trees, and Spanish moss, surrounding alligator-filled swamps: in short, guerrilla country, unsuited to pitched battle. The forest is approached today by U.S. Highway 17 north of the elegant and historic city of Charleston.

The **Congaree Swamp National Monument** consists of 15,135 acres of bottomland in the center of the state. Twenty miles southeast of Columbia on South Carolina 48, the alluvial floodplain of the Congaree River is flanked by bluffs. The national monument is open daily, and guided canoe and walking tours may be arranged at weekends. Congaree forms the last important growth of virgin hardwood timber in the region. Conservation is also an important issue in other areas of the state. The **Carolina Sandhills National Wildlife Refuge**, near McBee on U.S. Highway 1, protects tree frogs and the red-cockaded woodpecker, typical species of the region. The **Santee National Wildlife Refuge** off U.S. Highway 301, is at the southern end of the Atlantic Flyway, and from its observation tower you may watch herons and egrets as well as wintering Canada geese. The **Cape Romain National Wildlife Refuge** borders the Francis Marion National Forest, along the coast. Saltmarsh, ponds, and woodland surround this former plantation, providing a home for snowy egrets, glossy ibises, and migratory wildfowl.

South of the Savannah River, Georgia is a cornerstone of the old south, the thirteenth original colony and the fourth state of the Union. The Appalachian range reaches it southernmost extreme in the north of the state. From Brasstown Bald Mountain, at 4,784 feet (1,457 m), the ridges descend to the Piedmont Plateau. Southward, the Dougherty Plain and Tifton Upland stretch toward the Florida state line and the Okefenokee Swamp. South of the port of Savannah the coastal inlets are surrounded by a gaggle of islands: Skidaway, Ossabaw, St. Catherine's, Sapelo, St. Simon's, Jekyll, and Cumberland – the Golden Isles.

The ridges along the state's northern border are clad by the hard woods of the **Chattahoochee National Forest**. Its 74,094 acres form two units. One lies to the west of Interstate 75, and is crossed by U.S. Highway 27 and Georgia 143. The other stretches westward all the way from U.S. Highway 411 to the wild and scenic Chattooga and the Tugaloo. The Chattahoochee Forest is a delightful area, its multitude of tree species being brightened in season by rhododendron and wildflowers. Its attractions include bosky waterfalls and streams. Visit the De Soto and Anna Ruby Falls areas, or fish for trout in the Cuhutta Wilderness. The backcountry harbors deer, wild boar, and bears. The smaller **Oconee National Forest** (114,220 acres) is crossed by U.S. Highway 278 and Georgia 15, north of Interstate 20. Both forests offer an ideal day's excursion, or longer camping holidays. Between them they have over 350 miles of trail for hikers or horse riders. Forty-eight miles of the Chattahoochee River have also been set aside as a national recreation area, offering further possibilities for countryside outings from the state capital. Atlanta, destroyed during the Civil War, is now a thriving city and large urban area.

The fauna of the Georgian central plateau land is protected in the **Piedmont National Wildlife Refuge.** Lying between the towns of Juliette and Round Oak (on U.S. Highway 23 and Georgia 11 respectively), the refuge's mixed woodland is home to red-cockaded woodpeckers, turkeys, and waterfowl. A long string of national wildlife refuges protects the remarkable creatures of the coastal inlets and islands like some federal Noah's arks: **Savannah, Tybee, Wassaw Island, Harris Neck, Blackbeard Island**, and **Wolf Island**. The habitats include marshes, woods, beaches, and dunes. The bird life is memorable for its brown pelicans, black skimmers, terns, and laughing gulls; for the cormorant-like anhinga; and for waders such as herons and egrets. Armor-plated armadillos, alligators, and loggerhead turtles complement the list of protected species. The **Cumberland Island National Seashore**

The flooding of South Carolina's Congaree River waters lush hardwood growth, and the Congaree Swamp National Monument includes stands of virgin forest. Here, bald cypress and tupelo are mixed with various hardwoods.

Overleaf: White clouds unfurl above the Atlantic horizon like giant spinnakers; beach grasses nod in the breeze, their roots helping to stabilize the dunes. Fifty-eight miles of the Outer Banks form Cape Lookout National Seashore.

The snowy egret is one of the many bird species protected at the Cape Romain National Wildlife Refuge, a wetland habitat on the edge of South Carolina's Francis Marion National Forest. The egrets are members of the heron family.

The anhinga is one of the strangest looking birds of the southeast, its weaving, reptilian neck giving it a second name – the snakebird. Its chief diet is fish, which it spears expertly with its pointed beak. Anhingas nest at Georgia's Harris Neck National Wildlife Refuge.

(36,978 acres) is accessible by boat or ferry from St. Mary's. This has to be one of the most beautiful of the coastal islands, with its lake, woods, dunes, and white sandy beaches.

There are many places in the United States where one feels a sense of history. In Georgia's **Okefenokee National Wildlife Refuge** one feels rather a sense of prehistory, of returning to the primordial slime. This extraordinary swamp stretches over 396,000 acres – a rank, often impenetrable wilderness of weeds and lilies, of bald cypress, live oak, gum trees, drooping Spanish moss, and insectivorous plants. Reptiles lurk in the Okefenokee: the deadly cottonmouth moccasin, the diamond back rattlesnake, treefrogs, turtles, and alligators. Otter, catfish, and longnose gar swim the brown waters, and flying squirrels and woodpeckers live in the trees. The St. Mary's River begins its journey to the Atlantic in the swamp, and the Suwanee flows southwest to the Gulf. Stephen C. Foster (1826–64) immortalized the "Swanee" in the song "The Old Folks at Home;" he also penned other anthems of the South, such as "O, Susanna" and "My Old Kentucky Home." The best time to visit Okefenokee is during the winter or spring. Primitive camping is available. The refuge is accessible via Georgia 177, south from Braganza, off U.S. Highway 1/23, and northeast from Fargo off U.S. Highway 441.

Florida is a world on its own, a land of lakes and rivers and swamps, of palm trees and golden beaches, of secluded keys and harbors. It is a beautiful place, and its balmy climate has attracted vacationers, real estate agents, and retired people. A coastal conurbation has been created along the southeastern coastal strip from Miami northward to West Palm Beach. Urbanization has also spread around Jacksonville, Orlando, St. Petersburg, and Tampa. Florida has changed indeed since the days when the Seminole Indians held sway, and pirates caroused along the keys. Fortunately, much of the state's landscape has survived intact; the protection of this remaining wilderness is of paramount importance for the ecosystem of the North American continent.

Florida has three national forests. The **Apalachicola** covers over half a million acres southwest of Tallahassee, primarily pine, cedar, and cypress. Its hardwood swamps are an unusual feature of the area. The **Osceola** is a fascinating cypress swamp, with its pines being forested commercially. Ocean Pond, bordered by Interstate 10 and approached from Olustee on U.S.90, is a popular recreational area. South on Interstate 75, an eastward turn onto Florida 40 leads across the **Ocala National Forest**, whose pines root in coarse sand. All three forests offer scope for open-air activities such as canoeing, fishing, hiking, and camping.

To the world, Cape Canaveral means only one thing: the John F. Kennedy Space Center. It was here that the space age began, and by now the sight of spectacular rocket launches is a familiar one to all of us. Less familiar is the coastline which stretches northward from the space center toward Daytona Beach. Twenty-five miles of barrier island were set aside as the **Canaveral National Seashore** in 1975. Part of its 57,627 acres remain under NASA administration. To the east, the blue seas and lacy white surf withdraws over glistening sands. To the west, the island encloses the quiet waters of the Mosquito Lagoon and the Indian River. The dunes are anchored by a variety of vegetation, including saw palmetto, sea oats, beach sunflower, and seagrape (the fruit of the latter provides a tasty morsel for raccoons). Other habitats within the park include stands of oak and pine, and mangrove swamps. Turtles scuttle seaward across the white sand and within the lagoon are manatees. These endangered, broad-tailed sirenians are thought to have given rise to the legends of mermaids and mermen. The shellfish of the region were being collected for food long ago, by the coastal Indians who were the first to

Overleaf: Sunset over Okefenokee, "land of the trembling earth." One of the most primitive tracts of land in the south, the Okefenokee is a huge peat bog, the home of wood duck and wading birds. At the chief entrance to the national wildlife refuge, the Suwannee Canal Reservation Area offers a chance to explore this mysterious world by canoe. For motorists and cyclists the Swamp Island Wildlife Observation Drive offers access to a boardwalk tour of the wetlands.

The southern sunshine: Palms line the dunes on the largest of the Golden Isles. The Cumberland Island National Seashore's headquarters is on the mainland at St. Mary's, on Georgia 40 east off Interstate 95. Information is available from here as well as from the Seacamp Visitor Center.

inhabit Canaveral. Their kitchen middens remain today. Canaveral is a fascinating juxtaposition of ancient history and futuristic technology. Surfers, swimmers, and sunbathers flock to Playalinda and Apollo beaches; the national seashore is open by day only, and camping is forbidden. Approach via U.S. Highway 1 and Florida 402.

The **Merritt Island National Wildlife Refuge** is contiguous with Canaveral, and protects a number of species whose survival is under threat: bald eagles, peregrine falcons, the Atlantic saltmarsh snake, and several turtles. A series of national wildlife refuges stretches southward down the peninsula and out to the Florida Keys: **Pelican Island, Hobe Sound, Loxahatchee, Great White Heron, Key West**. The **National Key Deer Refuge** supports the unique Florida Key deer.

One of the nation's most unusual parks lies off the Florida Keys – and most of it is underwater. The **Biscayne National Park** occupies 92,000 acres of ocean in Biscayne Bay, with a further 4,200 acres of land. This is made up of 32 tiny islands, which include Old Rhodes, Elliott, Sands, Adams, and Arsenicker Keys. These keys are fringed with dense mangrove, and shelter much wildlife. However, the true delights of the park are revealed once one dons a snorkel or scuba gear. For this is a coral reef, once the bane of Spanish galleons. Coral looks for all the world like a plant, but it is made up of normally colonial polyps which secrete a calcareous substance. This forms into a communal skeleton, which accretes over the years to form whole reefs and islands. Algae and marine plants colonize the fantastic coral formations, and tropical fish dart to and fro. This submarine wonderland never fails to amaze the diver. Access to the keys is by boat only. Park headquarters is on the mainland at Convoy Point, off U.S. Highway 1, east of Homestead. Elliott Key has a ranger station and a primitive campsite. To the south, the John Pennekamp State Park preserves another section of coral reef off Key Largo. And if diving and swimming seem a little too strenuous, both parks can be explored by special glass-bottomed boats.

Sea palmetto bristles along the Canaveral seashore, to the north of the Kennedy Space Center. The vegetation of the dunes is subtropical. The national seashore is popular with vacationers, who enjoy the golden beaches and rolling white breakers. Beachcombing reveals all kinds of shells: razors, angel wings, oysters, and cockles.

A diver examines elkhorn coral formations off the Florida keys. Biscayne and Pennekamp offer one of the nation's most exotic sights, beneath the waves. Coral reefs provide a habitat for multihued angelfish, parrotfish, and wrasse.

Overleaf: The setting sun casts its spell over the tranquil waters of the Florida coast. The John Pennekamp State Park and the Biscayne National Park are marine reservations, beautiful from the surface and spectacular underwater.

The southern tip of Florida is one of the world's most important wetlands, made up of the **Big Cypress National Preserve** (75,000 acres) and the **Everglades National Park** (1,400,533 acres). They do not exist in isolation, but are part of a complex network of waterways extending southward from Lake Okeechobee. The natural water flow has now been channeled and controlled. The system ensures the future of the wetlands, but it does mean that it relies entirely on the capriciousness of human planning decisions. Big Cypress, a vast swamp of cypress which blooms with orchids and exotic flowers, plays a crucial role in this delicate balance. Its fresh waters slowly percolate through the Everglades. *Pa-hay-okee*, which means "grassy waters," is the Miccosukee Indian name for the Everglades. A visitor to Pa-hay-okee Overlook in the park will understand the description: a wide expanse of beardgrass, Muhly grass, and saw grass, the latter a rasp-bladed sedge, lies before one. Little islands ("hammocks") arise from this, enclaves of hardwoods such as mahogany. Saltmarshes, mangrove swamps, stands of pine and cypress, lakes, ponds, and sloughs all make up the incredible mosaic of the

Wetland vegetation of the Everglades. Florida's best known national park is of incalculable importance to the ecology of the southern states, and has been designated a World Heritage Site and an International Biosphere Reserve. Its survival depends upon human management of resources.

Everglades ecosystem. Many of the plants are tropical species, native to the Caribbean region. The southern coast of the Everglades fragments into the bewildering maze of banks and keys known as Florida Bay. The western perimeter of the park encloses the aptly named Ten Thousand Island region.

Perhaps the most important feature of the park is its wildlife. Its alligators are the best known, rescued from the brink of destruction at the hands of hunters. The nests of these magnificent, savage creatures abound within the park. The estuarine crocodile is a scarcer relative, a green-scaled hunter of the coasts. Mammals include the rare Florida panther, the whitetailed deer, the mink, the manatee, and the dolphin, schools of which leap playfully offshore. The tree snails of the Everglades are unique, noted for the brightly coloured rings around their shells. Bird life is spectacular: Egrets and roseate spoonbills are the Everglades' most elegant inhabitants. Wood storks and herons nest here, and Everglades' kites, bald eagles, and osprey can be observed. Some of the snakes in the park are venomous, notably the water moccasin, the coral snake, and the diamondback rattlesnake.

Winter is the best time to visit the Everglades; in the summer insect bites can be a nuisance. Miami is the obvious base for exploring the region. U.S. Highway 41 leads west to the Oasis Ranger Station of Big Cypress and to the Florida 29 turn-off to Everglades City. Here is the Everglades' Gulf Coast Ranger Station. U.S. Highway 1 and Route 997

Stands of pine rise from dense palmetto in the Everglades National Park. The shallow, peaty soil overlies limestone. It supports a wide range of vegetation from marshland grasses to forest.

(formerly Florida 27) lead to Florida City. From here, travel west on 9336 to the main visitor center. This road crosses the wetlands, terminating at the Flamingo Visitor Center. Hiking trails vary from ½ mile to 14 miles. Fishing is a popular pastime, the catch including saltwater fish such as snook, snapper, and redfish. Freshwater fishing for largemouth bass requires a state license. The creeks and swamps may be explored by tour boat, canoe, or small motorboat. A "wilderness waterway" weaves in and out of the Gulf coast sector, calling at campsites on the way. Camping is popular, but permits are needed for the backcountry. Accommodation is available at Flamingo Lodge.

Conservation projects continue along Florida's Gulf coast at a series of national wildlife refuges: **J.N. "Ding" Darling, Egmont Key, Chassahowitzka, Cedar Keys, Lower Suwanee, St. Mark's,** and **St. Vincent.** The **Gulf Islands National Seashore** comprises 65,817 acres of shoreline and offshore islands. To historians the area is of interest for its ancient Amerindian settlements, its colonial history, and its nineteenth-century military fortifications. The islands act as a barrier against the powerful hurricanes which regularly assault this coast. Their white sand dunes are colonized by sea oats, palmetto, stunted live oaks, and slash pine. The sound thus enclosed is a nursery for shrimps and other crustaceans. The coastal habitat is typical of the bayou country: marshland, with loblolly pine and hardwoods. Regional fauna includes armadillos, opossums, raccoons, bullfrogs, rattlesnakes, and alligators;

surf anglers catch pompano, seatrout, and mackerel. Naturalists love this seashore, and scuba diving reveals the secrets of the ocean floor. The park has several separate sections. The Florida unit surrounds Pensacola Bay. Here is the Naval Live Oaks section, approached by bridge on U.S. Highway 98. Continue southward from here to Santa Rosa Island and Fort Pickens. Across the bay, to the west of the air base, is Fort Barrancas, a flashpoint during the Civil War. West of Perdido Key, one sails past Alabama's Mobile Bay before park territory resumes across the Mississippi line. Here the Davis Bayou section is approached by Hanley Road off U.S. Highway 90. The barrier islands here are Petit Bois, Horn, and East and West Ship. The latter may be reached aboard a passenger excursion boat from Biloxi or Gulfport.

From Mobile Bay the hinterland of Alabama backs onto the Florida panhandle. Its humid plains are interrupted by the Red Hills and the twin streams of the Tombigbee and the Alabama rivers. The Chattahoochee forms the southern part of the Georgia line. The north of the state is crossed by the dammed reaches of the Tennessee River and the uplands of the Cumberland Plateau.

The National Forest Service administers four areas in Alabama. The **Conecuh Forest** covers 84,000 acres on the Florida line, which is here breached by the river of the same name. This is a working forest of southern pine which contains the luxuriant subtropical flora of the coastal plain. The **Tuskagee National Forest** lies west of Montgomery,

The Gulf Islands National Seashore parallels the coasts of Florida and Mississippi over a distance of 150 miles. West Ship lies on the Mississippi Sound, ten miles off Biloxi. Summer visitors may enjoy swimming and guided tours of historic Fort Massachusetts.

south off Interstate 85. It is a small forest of 11,000 acres, but its rolling pine-clad hills form a pleasant backdrop to its hiking trails. Camping is available. **Talladega National Forest** (371,258 acres) includes the highest point in Alabama, Cheaha Mountain (2,907 feet; 734 m). This mixed forest forms two separate units, the Talladega and the Oakmulgee. The Talladega Scenic Drive offers striking views of the hill country. The **William B. Bankhead National Forest** (179,539 acres) surrounds the L.M. Smith Reservoir, to the west of Interstate 5. Virgin hardwood forest is still to be found here, and rocky cliffs, river canyon, and waterfalls may be viewed from the trails. Camping, boating, fishing, and swimming are all allowed in the forest.

On Alabama's western border, the Chattahoochee River spills into the Walter F. George Reservoir. The **Eufaula National Wildlife Refuge**, off U.S. Highway 431, includes varying terrain from marshes to woodland. Gallinules (members of the rail family) step out across the banks, and many other water birds can be seen through binoculars. At the opposite end of the state the **Choctaw National Wildlife Refuge,** on the Tombigbee River, offers security to woodland birds and mammals. Wheeler Lake is on the Tennessee River in the north of the state. To the east of Interstate 65 the **Wheeler National Wildlife Refuge** sees an annual invasion of Canada geese and other waterfowl. The **Russell Cave National Monument** (310 acres) is sited near the Tennessee state line; approach from Bridgeport off U.S. Highway 72. This huge cavern was

The Everglades' most famous inhabitant, the alligator. Fish, turtles, and mammals are included in its diet. Protection of the Everglades has led to a respite for the alligator, whose skin was prized by hunters and used for shoes and handbags. Today its chances of survival have improved considerably.

occupied by Indian cave-dwellers over nine millennia. Its extraordinary history has been uncovered by archeologists, and a guided tour brings one face to face with a sobering span of history.

Mississippi occupies a narrow section of the Gulf coast between the Pearl River and Petit Bois Island. Inland the border backtracks on Louisiana to the Mississippi River itself, which it follows northward to the Tennessee state line below Memphis. The southern plain is criss-crossed by rivers and extends back beyond the Southern Pine Hills to Jackson Prairie, the Yazoo, and the northern lakes.

Near the Mississippi unit of the Gulf Islands National Seashore, 16,000 acres of countryside has been earmarked for conservation. This is the habitat of the threatened Mississippi sandhill crane, a stately fawn-plumaged bird with a red cap; it may be observed at the **Mississippi Sandhill Crane National Wildlife Refuge**. A cluster of refuges in the center of the state harbors deer, beaver, fox, wild turkey, and waterfowl in their bottomlands: **Yazoo**, **Panther Swamp**, **Hillside**, **Morgan Brake**, **Mathews Brake**, and **Noxubee**.

The **De Soto National Forest** (499,863 acres) occupies part of sunny southern Mississippi, a lazy, lovely woodland of rivers, lakes, and bottomlands. Hike the 20-mile Tuxachanie Trail or take a leisurely 24-mile float trip. De Soto is quartered by Mississippi 26 and U.S. Highway 49. Camping and outdoor pursuits are encouraged. The **Homochitto National Forest** (188,994 acres) is a working forest of the deep South, located near Natchez. The **Bienville National Forest**, east of Jackson on Interstate 20/U.S. Highway 80, includes virgin forest and boasts three recreational areas. Mississippi's western forest is the **Delta**, a bottomland flooded seasonally. This is the most productive hardwood forest in the nation. **Tombigbee National Forest** (two sites totaling 66,457 acres) is mixed woodland running through hill country. De Soto set up his winter quarters near Davis Lake. Indian mounds are to be seen here, and the Natchez Trace Parkway follows the old trading route from Natchez to Nashville, Tennessee. The **Holly Springs National Forest** (149,623 acres) comprises two northern forests and takes in Chewalla Lake.

Louisiana is one of the South's most charming states, a historic and beautiful region which has retained its traditions and relaxed way of life. This spirit is epitomized in New Orleans, the birthplace of jazz. New Orleans' colonial influence is evident in the decorative, elegant architecture and the shady courtyards. The French language is still to be heard. Northward from the great delta, the steamy Mississippi forms the state's eastern border, while its tributary, the Red River, swings in from the west. The Sabine and the Toledo Bend Reservoir form the state's western border.

The Mississippi Delta is one of the most important of the Gulf's many wetland areas. These regions are of the greatest benefit to human society as well as to wildlife, and have protected the coastal plains for thousands of years. In our own century we have interfered with nature's status quo, by polluting the waters, and by dredging and draining the swamps. The Mississippi Delta region alone lost over 20 percent of its marshes in post-war years. A growing awareness of the international significance of the Gulf Wetlands has aroused a greater understanding in recent years. The **Delta National Wildlife Refuge** (48,799 acres) lies in the midst of this labyrinthine network of channels, bayous, and ponds. Oil and natural gas, the mainstays of the Gulf economy, are extracted in the vicinity, but the problems have been minimized by careful planning. The tangled vegetation and oozing waters see tens of thousands of snowgeese winter here, along with other geese and duck, at the bottom of the great Mississippi flyway. In all, 239 species of bird have been recorded here over the years. The **Breton National Wildlife Refuge** (9,000 acres) is in the northeast of the Delta region, and takes in the Chandeleur Islands as well as the two Breton Islands. This too is a wintering ground for many different species of waterfowl, and a summer breeding site for terns, gulls, and skimmers. Other Louisiana reserves include **Lacassine**,

White sands and the waters of the Gulf off Mississippi's Ship Island. Passenger ferries journey to the mainland and back during the summer season. Private vessels may moor near Fort Massachusetts by day throughout the year. The barrier islands buffer the Gulf coast from hurricanes.

The Russell Cave National Monument in northeastern Alabama, near the Tennessee line. For thousands of years this locality was settled by Indian peoples: A visit reveals the long history of the southern states prior to European settlement.

A young sandhill crane. Sandhill cranes have suffered less at the hands of hunters than their close relatives the whooping cranes. The habitat of the endangered Mississippi sandhill crane is protected in a special reserve near Gautier.

Sabine, Catahoula, and **Upper Ouachita** national wildlife refuges.

Northwest of Baton Rouge, the **Kisatchie National Forest** takes care of 597,038 acres of varied landscape in its eight separate sections. Dank swamps swill over part of the region, the red, fibrous bark of the bald cypress being festooned with Spanish moss. *Magnolia grandiflora*, the official state flower, blooms elsewhere, and dark green pines scent sunny hillsides. The forest is popular with visitors, who come to camp, fish, or walk the trails. Spring and fall are the best seasons in which to visit Kisatchie.

Arkansas takes its name from the great river which crosses it eastward, joining the Mississippi on the state's eastern border. The river snakes its way between the Ouachita and Boston mountains, in the high country of the northwest. One of the most scenic waterways in Arkansas is the **Buffalo National River**. A park of 87,883 acres surrounds 132 miles of its banks. The sparkling, translucent waters stream through bluffs of weathered limestone, offering exciting canoe trips. Along the banks you can hike, camp, or simply stop off for a picnic and admire the wholesome Ozark countryside.

The state of Arkansas can claim within its bounds the first land in the nation to be placed under federal care, in 1832. **Hot Springs National Park** (4,826 acres) lies near the junction of U.S. Highways 270 and 70

Arkansas: The Ouachita landscape extends into the distant haze, blanketed with rolling green forests. The Ouachita National Forest lies in the west of the state.

and Arkansas 7, southwest of Little Rock. Interstate 30 passes 22 miles westward. As its name suggests, this is a spa: 47 springs of pure water well up from the depths of the earth, reaching temperatures of up to 142°F (62°C). Therapeutic bathing is today as popular as ever, and the springs are used to this end. Two springs may be viewed by the public, who may also care to hike the park's trails, which pass through forested mountain scenery.

To the west of Hot Springs, the largest forest in Arkansas stretches across the Oklahoma Line. The **Ouachita National Forest** (1,585,264 acres) with its gum, hickory, oak, maple, and sycamore is well known for its colorful fall displays. The trees rise from the slopes of the Ouachita Mountains and neighboring ranges. The Ouachita River offers floating, along a spectacular and varied stretch of water. The mountains are perhaps best viewed from Talamena Scenic Drive. In the north of the state, the **Ozark National Forest** (1,119,000 acres) is another area of singular beauty. It incorporates the Upper Buffalo Wilderness Area.

Every year thousands of migrating ducks and geese fly over Arkansas, and national wildlife refuges have been set up to afford them safe passage and wintering grounds. **White River**, **Wapanocca**, and **Big Lake** are in the east; **Felsenthal** is in the south; and **Holla Bend** is in central Arkansas.

The elegant bloom of the iris, an example of Louisiana's splendid flora. The iris is a rhizomatous plant favoring a damp habitat. The state includes important areas of wetland.

The Midwest

Illinois, Indiana, Iowa, Kansas, Michigan, Minnesota, Missouri, Nebraska, North Dakota, Ohio, South Dakota, Wisconsin

The prairie dog is a burrowing rodent typical of the North American grassland regions. Treated for years as troublesome pests, prairie dogs in fact play a very important role in maintaining a prairie habitat, by breaking down the soil. They live in colonies known as "towns," which consist of underground passages and chambers.

Opposite: Alley Spring lies beneath a cliff on the Jacks Fork section of the Ozark National Scenic Riverways. The 81 million gallons of water it supplies daily were harnessed for power at the end of the last century by the building of Red Mill. This charming building is still standing today.

St. Louis, Missouri, was built at the hub of the continent, for here the waters of the Missouri, flowing eastward from the Rockies, join forces with the southward-bound Mississippi to form one mighty stream. From the banks of both great rivers a maze of tributaries extend east and west, the warp and weft of the nation. The lands west of the Ohio River and north of the Ozark plateaux are normally defined as the Midwest, a historical term which reflects the perceptions of early settlers on the eastern seaboard rather than the region's evident centrality. Like a grasping hand, the Great Lakes claw into the region, the fingers of Superior and Michigan prodding west and south. Erie, Huron, and Superior form a natural border with Canada, but to the west this frontier is drawn with a ruler right across the continent. The region enjoys some diversity of terrain, with low hills, lakes, and streams; many rivers have been dammed to create reservoirs. The most apparent feature of the Midwest, however, is its flatness: an area of open prairie or grassy plain.

These grasslands once fed countless herds of wild bison and were rich in game. Native peoples farmed and hunted, until under the pressure of European intrusion into the area Indian tribes were forced to move. The Dakota, for example, known to settlers as the Sioux, moved westward from their homelands in the region of Lake Superior. On the Great Plains to the west a new culture evolved, based around the hunting of the bison. The first whites in the region were mostly French: trappers, explorers, and soldiers, trying to outflank the Engish colonial hegemony along the east coast. French names remain today: Fond du Lac, La Crosse, Eau Claire, Des Moines, and Terre Haute.

Following independence from Britain, the new republic rapidly gained control of this backwoods territory, and settlers poured westward, the first in a flood that was to engulf the continent. Conflict was not restricted to Indian wars. The bitterness of the Civil War period scarred the early history of these new states. Abraham Lincoln had spent his formative years in southwestern Indiana, and thundered his opposition to slavery from Illinois' political platforms. The Indian nations such as the Sioux, Pawnee, and Cheyenne were confined to reservations, and even more settlers arrived from Europe and from the ravaged South. Huge cities grew up: Cleveland, Cincinnatti, Chicago, Detroit. To the west, farmers suffered periodically from hardship before the advent of modern techniques and the development of agriculture as an important industry. The prairies were no longer wild grassland but enormous tracts of wheat, voraciously consumed by combine harvesters.

Today, the Midwest remains an area of intense economic activity, with industry centered upon the eastern north-central states, which have a population density of 170.9 per square mile. The agricultural western north-central states have a density of only 33.8 per square mile. The mineral resources of Michigan, Ohio, and Indiana include coal. Detroit

is an important lakeside port and center for the automobile industry. Chicago is the principal center of manufacture and processing, with an important commercial and services sector. The Midwest's agricultural products include wheat, soybeans, maize, oats, and root crops such as potatoes and beet. The farmer's problems today are not so much floods, droughts, or plagues of grasshoppers, but the vagaries of the international grain market. The raising of beef cattle is as important as ever, and Wisconsin is noted for its dairy herds.

Intensive farming, mining, industrialization, and urbanization have radically changed the midwestern landscape in the last 100 years. Pollution has become a major problem, with chemical effluent poisoning the rivers of the east. And yet, despite all this, a new ecological consciousness has arisen, determined to mitigate the effects of past mistakes and to plan the future more carefully. Happily, the Midwest has in many places retained its age-old beauty and the sweeping grandeur of the open plains.

The state animal of Kansas is the American bison; the official tree, the cottonwood; the flower, the helianthus (a wild indigenous sunflower); and the state bird is the western meadow lark. These represent flora and fauna typical of Kansas grassland, although the days of the vast herds of bison are gone with the likes of Iowa-born Bill Cody (1846–1917). "Buffalo" Bill slaughtered 5,000 of these creatures in just 18 months, when employed to supply meat to workers on the Kansas Pacific Railway. Since Mennonite farmers introduced the hardy wheats of Russia to Kansas in the last century, the natural grasses have largely been replaced by grain crops; the open prairie is now dissected by a geometrical grid of roads. Kansas today symbolizes the American heartland, its expanses of golden corn stirring under the blue skies and driving white clouds of summer. Sometimes, however, nature presents a more terrifying aspect, and a tornado winds across the landscape under a lowering sky. Cattle are raised by Kansas farmers as well as crops, and the low, rolling Flint Hills provide a rich pasture of big bluestem grass, Indian grass, needlegrass, and blue grama.

Kansas has 22 state parks, which preserve many of the more beautiful landscapes of the state, and which offer a home to prairie dog, badger, fox, and deer. The largest federally protected unit in the state is the **Cimarron National Grassland**, 108,175 acres of plain in the southwestern corner. This rolling prairie may be reached via Kansas 27 off U.S. Highway 56. The Cimarron River flows across open country before looping westward and then south to cross the Oklahoma line. Lesser prairie chickens are native to this habitat, as are bobwhite and scaled quail. Ruminants include pronghorns and deer. The best time to visit Cimarron is during early summer or fall.

Many of the rivers of Kansas have been dammed, and large reservoirs offer opportunities for boating, fishing, camping, and walking. Webster, Kirwin, Glen Elder, Wilson, Milford, Tuttle Creek, and Perry reservoirs are in the north of the state; Kanopolis, Marion, and John Redmond in the center; Cheney, Fall River and Elk City in the south. The 10,778-acre **Kirwin National Wildlife Refuge** (off Kansas 9) is an enclosure of grassland and trees surrounding a reservoir at the confluence of Bow Creek with the north fork of the Solomon. As winter draws in, large flocks of honking Canada geese arrive for the molting season: They are recognized by their black bills and feet, black neck with white chin, and black-and-white tail feathers. Other waterfowl include teal, mallard, and pintails. The **Quivira National Wildlife Refuge** is situated on Rattlesnake Creek, southeast of Great Bend, in the center of the state. Its 21,820 acres combine a mixture of habitats: stands of timber, sandhills, and wetlands. Golden and bald eagles are attracted to this site, along with Mississippi kites and white pelicans. Mammal species include badgers and coyotes. The John Redmond Reservoir, 140 miles due east of Quivira, is formed by the damming of the Neosho River southeast of

Emporia. Its flood plain takes in both prairie and agricultural land, and 18,463 acres form the **Flint Hills National Wildlife Refuge.** This too is on the flight path of migrating waterfowl, including the snowgoose (largely white, with pink feet and bill) and the white-fronted goose (a brown bird with a white surround to its bill). Nature trails and camping are available at all the above sites with the exception of Quivira.

Across the great Missouri, further national wildlife refuges protect migratory bird species. **Swan Lake** (10,670 acres south of Pershing State Park) is famous for its annual influx of Canada geese, while the **Squaw Creek National Wildlife Refuge** (6,837 acres near Mound City) is a vital piece in the ecological jigsaw, for in winter it plays host to a large population of bald eagles, the magnificent white-headed predators which are an endangered species and the official symbol of the United States. In the southeast, the marshes and woodlands of the **Mingo National Wildlife Refuge** (21,676 acres near Puxico) also attract bald eagles as well as wild turkeys.

The National Forest Service lands in the state of Missouri come under the administration of the **Mark Twain National Forest,** 1,500,000 acres of mixed forest and open grassland in the Ozark region. Its 13 separate units are a tribute to the more enlightened environmentalists of our day, and a fitting memorial to one of America's best-loved writers. Nineteenth-century mining methods ravaged these hills, and lumber operators and agriculture created a dustbowl. In 1933 conservation and reclamation began in earnest, and today's mining operations fit into a more traditional landscape, and contribute toward its upkeep. Hike through the Ozarks amid a tangle of oak, hickory, pine, and cedar; you can camp, fish, swim, or ride the trails on horseback.

The most exciting way to explore southern Missouri is by canoe or john boat. The **Ozark National Scenic Riverways** (80,788 acres) include 100 miles of the Current and 34 miles of the Jacks Fork rivers. Smallmouth and largemouth bass, bluegill, and walleye are fished in these waters, and paddling your way downstream you experience the

Wind and water have carved these ancient sandstone heights into strange humps. The Garden of the Gods is in the eastern part of the Shawnee National Forest, in Illinois. A trail system winds among the rocks and the beautiful woods.

Ozarks much as the early explorers did. The geology of the area is fascinating. Porous limestone caps non-porous granite. Seeping rainwater has dissolved the limestone into caves, tunnels, and sinkholes, and underground springs well up in profusion. In many places stalactites and stalagmites have been formed in the caves. The wealth of spring and summer wildflowers include spring beauty, sweet william, wild geranium, oxeye daisy, blazing star, and golden rod. The combination of dense woodland with a riparian habitat attract bobcat, deer, squirrels, barred owls, green herons, whippoorwills, and many other wild creatures. Bats occupy many of the caves. Visitors to the Riverways may approach southward from Interstate 44 to Salem or from U.S. Highway 60 at Van Buren. The region is crossed by scenic roads such as Missouri 19 and 106. Montauk State Park to the north is famous for its trout streams. Other attractions include Round Spring, Powder Mill (for its ferry and visitor center), Alley Spring, Blue Spring, and Welch Spring. This fresh world of brimming rivers, green in spring and golden in fall, offers days of relaxation. Camping is available throughout the region, with major grounds at Alley Springs, Akers, Round Spring, and Pulltite. River travelers may camp midstream on the gravel bars.

The Illinois border follows the course of the Mississippi-Missouri system. These rivers are just as vital for wildlife as they have been for humankind throughout history. In recognition of this fact the **Mark Twain National Wildlife Refuge** has been created to ensure safe passage to the great flocks of migratory waterfowl which rely on it. Its 23,500 acres overlap three states – Illinois, Iowa and Missouri. In central Illinois the **Chautauqua National Wildlife Refuge** offers an additional haven, as does **Crab Orchard** in the south.

The latter lies in the northern part of the **Shawnee National Forest,** whose 255,984 acres are crossed by Interstates 57 and 24, by U.S. Highways 51 and 45, and by Illinois 13. The forest's western border runs parallel to the Mississippi River. The eastern border is formed by the Ohio River. The entire forest is traversed by the River-to-River Trail, a 47-mile hike across ridges of pine, oak, hickory, redbud, and dogwood. During the Ice Ages, the forest was the home of mastodon and mammoth. In 8,000 B.C. nomadic groups of Amerindians were hunting the area; later Indian tribes developed a more sophisticated culture, trading, warring or defending stone forts. Indian mounds and wall drawings may still be seen. Indians first saw white explorers in the seventeenth century, and later became involved in the rivalry between the two colonial powers. The Trail of Tears crosses the southern section of Shawnee, marking the most tragic chapter in the history of the Cherokee nation. The forest was established in 1933 as an attempt to reclaim an exhausted landscape. The bid was successful and a lovely part of the Midwest has now been restored to its former glory. The land is varied, including canyons and ridges, creeks, lakes, and springs. Within the park is the LaRue-Pine Hills Ecological Area, devoted to the preservation of rare species, and many nature trails. The forest-dwellers include woodchuck, gray and fox squirrels, bobcat, and whitetailed deer. Over a third of all North American bird species have been spotted here over the years: waterbirds such as loons, herons, duck, and geese; hawks, kites, and eagles; turkey vultures (known familiarly as "buzzards"); flycatchers; woodpeckers; vireos; warblers; and many others. The Oakwood Bottoms Greentree Reservoir is an oak forest flooded with water every winter. The Garden of the Gods – sandstone bluffs eroded by wind and water – is another point of interest. Motorists obtain excellent views of the forest from the Pinehills Skyline Drive and the Fountain Bluff Scenic Drive. The Shawnee is ideal for backpackers, hikers, naturalists, climbers, cyclists, campers, and horse riders. Information may be obtained at the ranger stations in Elizabethtown, Murphysboro, Jonesboro, and Vienna.

Across the Wabash River lies the state of Indiana, and the **Hoosier National Forest** (180,064 acres). Once upon a time Indiana was one of

the world's largest hardwood suppliers. Lack of forest management led to a decimation of the natural forest, of which Hoosier is a remnant. Half a century of National Forest Service care has made amends, and today the two units of this picturesque forest are well worth a visit. Ranger stations at Tell City and Brownstown will give information about recreational facilities such as camping, fishing, and hiking. West of the Hoosier Forest the **Muscatuck National Wildlife Refuge** (7,702 acres) near Seymour supports waterfowl and deer.

The **Indiana Dunes National Lakeshore** give the visitor some idea of what Lake Michigan must have been like before the concrete canyon-lands of Chicago overran its shores. Situated off U.S. Highway 12 between Gary and Michigan City, the 12,535-acre site features high dunes and sandy beaches, with a hinterland of thick wood, marsh, and open grassland. The restoration of historical buildings within the park area has complemented the unspoiled landscape.

South of Lake Erie, the state of Ohio has been sorely used by generations who made their wealth from it. The native broadleaved forest was cleared for farmland by the first white settlers, and the landscape subsequently farmed and mined to exhaustion. In 1951 the **Wayne National Forest** was established to heal the scars and restore the balance of nature. Its 176,000 acres are divided into three main sections. The southernmost is crossed by Ohio 93 and 233, and U.S. Highway 52; the central section straddles Ohio 216, 93, 78, and U.S. Highway 33 the eastern section surrounds Ohio 7, 26, and 800. The central section has smaller satellite forests to the southwest and southeast. Headquarters is in Bedford; ranger offices are located in Ironton and Athens and there is a visitor center at Lake Vesuvius. The forest provides recreation areas for the big cities of the east, with camping, riding, cycling, and boating.

The month of May on the Indiana Dunes National Lakeshore, and the delicate stars of sand phlox brighten the Cowles Bog area. Marsh and forest zones back onto the dunes of Lake Michigan.

Hikers may walk the Vesuvius Trail (16 miles), and industrial archaeologists will be interested in the Hanging Rock region as the site of iron production during the Civil War period. In northern Ohio, the **Cuyahoga Valley National Recreation Area** provides a welcome interlude of green countryside between Akron and Cleveland. The tightly meandering river threads its way through meadows and woods of oak and maple which in fall are transformed into a canopy of scarlet and gold. The Erie region of northern Ohio is important for migrating waterfowl and waders, and a haven for them is provided at the **Ottawa National Wildlife Refuge** near Oak Harbor.

The state of Michigan lies at the heart of the Great Lakes, which were formed by gigantic glaciers during the last Ice Age. Although Michigan has major urban areas such as Detroit, Lansing, and Grand Rapids, it also has over 2¾ million acres of pine and hardwood forests including the **Hiawatha, Huron, Manistee**, and **Ottawa** national forests. The **Shiawassee National Wildlife Refuge** around the headwaters of the Saginaw is visited by flocks of migrant swans in spring, and across the Mackinac Straits the large **Seney National Wildlife Refuge** consists of 95,455 acres of islands, lakes, and woods. The Great Manistique Swamp is an important nesting ground for thousands of birds.

A chipmunk scampers through a stand of maple in Ohio. The state forests include a wide variety of hardwood species. Sugar maple is common in the northeast of the state. Is is valued for its timber and also for its sap, the basic ingredient of maple syrup. Early settlers learned the secret of syrup-making from the Indians.

90

The **Sleeping Bear Dunes National Lakeshore** (70,983 acres) is a
world of reflected light and shifting sands, on the eastern shore of Lake
Michigan. Here glacial moraine has created bluffs which rise to a height
of 460 feet (140 m) above the water, and these have accumulated vast hills
of white (predominantly quartz) sand, which have worked their way
inland, covering old settlements and forests. The name "sleeping bear"
comes from Chippewan folklore: A mother bear once swam to this shore
with her two cubs. They failed to reach dry land and drowned; she
scanned the horizon for them in vain, until falling into eternal sleep.
Today her resting place is marked by a large dune, while the cubs'
memorial is formed by the twin offshore islands of North and South
Manitou. Sleeping Bear is a "perched dune," atop a bluff. To the
southwest, Platte Bay's Aral Dunes are at shore level. Lake Michigan's
dunes are colonized and stabilized by coarse marram grass, sand cherry,
wormwood, ground juniper, and cottonwood. Inland the landscape
changes to one of beech and maple forest, still lakes and peaceful rivers.
The park's wildlife includes gulls, sandpipers, and turnstones, rodents
hunted by red-shouldered hawks and foxes, and hognose snakes.
Walkers might care to comb the lakeshore for driftwood or shells, or
hike the short Empire Bluff Trail. Motorists can best view the area from
the Pierce Stocking Scenic Drive. Camping is available, and
opportunities for outdoor activities range from sailing and angling to
cross-country skiing in winter. The visitor center is on Michigan 109
south of Glen Lake. Michigan 22 links with the Platte River section in the
south, and with Leland to the north-east. A passenger ferry plies
between Leland and South Manitou Island, which also has a visitor
center.

Munising is a town on the state's upper peninsula, reached by
Michigan 28 and 94. Between here and Grand Marais (on Michigan 77),
another section of coastline invites exploration. The **Pictured Rocks
National Lakeshore**, 71,400 acres on the shores of Lake Superior, was
the first to be so designated. A former hunting ground of the Ojibway
Indians, the area underwent extensive deforestation in the late nineteenth
century at the hands of commercial operatives. However, in our own day

*Massive banks of white sand characterize
Sleeping Bear Dunes on the shores of Lake
Michigan. The national lakeshore takes in
a wide variety of environments, including
woods, farmland, and inland lakes.*

Miner's Castle, on the Pictured Rocks
National Lakeshore in Michigan.
Alongside the waters of Lake Superior, a
trail takes one past weathered cliffs and
along open beaches. The colorful rocks are
eroded in places into arches and caverns.

Dawn illuminates the skyline of Isle Royale National Park in Keweenaw County. Davidson Island is part of this wild, unspoiled group of islands in Lake Superior.

a narrow strip of hinterland is resplendent with birch, hemlock, spruce, fir, and pine. Hiking trails lead to rivers, lakes, and waterfalls. The shoreline itself is skirted by the Lakeshore Trail. From the Munising Visitor Center it leads to the Sand Point headquarters. Past the Miner's Castle are the Pictured Rocks themselves, eroded cliffs of warmly colored sandstone which rise to a maximum height of about 200 feet (60 m). Beyond Grand Portal Point, hikers can stride out along the sand and pebbles of Twelvemile Beach, before crossing the Hurricane River to reach the high duneland of Grand Sable, and then the eastern visitor center. The rocks may be viewed by boat. Camping is available, and permits are needed for backcountry trekkers. Winter sports' followers can try snowshoeing, cross-country skiing, and ice-fishing.

The wildest part of Michigan, indeed some of the least spoiled territory in the Great Lakes region, is the **Isle Royale National Park,** a 571,796-acre island site in Lake Superior. Visitors must approach the archipelago by boat or floatplane. On arrival they will find themselves isolated in a world without cars or roads, so they will have to be prepared to paddle a canoe or hike the forest trails. In its day the island has known French trappers and Chippewa Indians, prospectors, lumberjacks, and tourists. Today the mixed forest and sparkling inlets are the preserve of the animal kingdom: moose, timber wolf, squirrel, fox, and beaver. Visitors arrive on Isle Royale by boat from Grand Portage, Minnesota, or by air or boat from Haughton. Accommodation and camping is available; information is available from Rock Harbor, Mott Island, and Windigo. The park is closed during the bitterly cold winter months.

The map of Wisconsin looks as if it is spilling over with quicksilver. Rivers run hither and thither, dividing and draining into great waterways such as the Mississippi. Lakes of all sizes brim with shining water. Four hundred or more of them are to be found in the **Chequamon National Forest** alone. This is the home of hardwoods and of spruce and pine, taking up three sites totalling 847,000 acres in the north of the state. The **Nicolet National Forest**, to the east, has pine, birch, and sugar maple, the official state tree, whose fall foliage is every bit as amazing as the sweet taste of its sap, used to make maple syrup. Over 66,000 acres of

Typical vegetation of the Canadian border: Boreal conifer forest lines the lakeshore in Michigan's Isle Royale National Park. The federal frontier crosses Lake Superior to the north of Isle Royale.

A water-bound wilderness: Malone Bay in the Isle Royale National Park lies leaden beneath a troubled sky. The waters of Lake Superior can be bitterly cold.

Wisconsin are preserved with its wildlife in mind. National wildlife refuges are to be found at **Necedah**, in the center of the state; at **Horicon**, in the southeast; and at **Trempealeau**, northwest of La Crosse on the banks of the Mississippi. The fauna of Wisconsin includes ruffed grouse, woodpeckers, sandhill cranes, waterfowl, foxes, deer, badgers, muskellunge, walleye, and crappie.

The **Apostle Islands National Lakeshore** occupies 42,009 acres in the far north of the state. It encompasses part of the Bayfield Peninsula and the 20 wooded islands of the Apostle Archipelago. Wisconsin 13, east from Duluth, Minnesota, leads to the region, and boat trips take you to the islands, the largest of which is Madeline. The mainland visitor center is located at Sand Bay, northwest of Bayfield. Fine beaches and cliffs of sandstone rise from the ever-changing waters of Lake Superior. Camping is available on the islands. Walking, boating, and offshore fishing are popular pastimes. The coast of Lake Superior and the landscape of Wisconsin was originally formed by glaciation. Nine sites of special interest to geologists have been brought together under the umbrella of the **Ice Age National Scientific Reserve**, established in 1964. Locations include Cross Plains, Devil's Lake, Campbellsport Drumlins, Kettle Moraine, Sheboygan Marsh, Mill Bluff, Two Creeks Buried Forest, Chippewa Moraine, and the Interstate Unit in the St. Croix region.

The St. Croix River rises in the watery maze of northwestern Wisconsin and travels southward, fed by the Namekegon and other tributaries before it joins with the Mississippi southeast of St. Paul. The Minnesota border accompanies much of its route. The **St. Croix National Scenic Riverway** is a canoeist's dream: Rapids contrast with more peaceful stretches of water, flowing through a forest of ash, maple, and oak, a rich hunting ground once fought over by the Sioux (Dakota) and the Chippewa. The river waters are the haunt of otter, mink, and

Wisconsin is bounded to the north by Lake Superior and to the east by Lake Michigan. Here at Cave Point the blue waters of Michigan lap the rugged lakeshore. The geology of the state is a legacy of ice age glaciation.

beaver, the pelts of the latter being much sought after in the days of the Hudson Bay Company. Trout, walleye, muskellunge, and bass are among the many species of fish which breed in the St. Croix and its tributaries, and herons and kingfishers grow sleek on the catch. Ninety-eight miles of the Namekegon and 102 miles of the St. Croix come under federal protection, and in summer many a visitor comes to camp, to float leisurely downstream, and to explore the backwoods. The visitor center is at St. Croix Falls. The **Lower St. Croix National Scenic Riverway** is a 27-mile extension south of Taylor's Falls, another marvelously scenic stretch of water popular for recreation.

Silver birches arch delicately over the easy-flowing river. The St. Croix National Scenic Riverway, lying between Wisconsin and Minnesota, is a place to paddle gently downstream, adapting one's pace to the timeless world of river and forest.

Previous page: Wisconsin is a patchwork of shining lakes and rivers, a wilderness best explored by canoe, in the tradition of the Chippewa Indians and the early French traders. This aerial view shows the St. Croix valley: The river flows south to form the Minnesota state line.

The quicksilver country of Wisconsin is reflected in the intricately etched lake system of Minnesota. From Lake of the Woods down to the Red Lakes, Winnibigoshish, Leech, and Mille Lacs, and southward, too, beyond the Mississippi and the Wisconsin, glaciation has left the surface of the earth pitted and flooded. Eight national wildlife refuges take advantage of this watery landscape to protect the infinite variety of wildlife which is dependent on it. Most notable is the **Upper Mississippi River National Wildlife and Fish Refuge**, 284 miles of preserve extending into three states, and the **Minnesota Wetlands Complex**, a 169,000-acre network of sites in the center and west of the state. In the north, the **Superior National Forest** includes some 2,000 lakes amid virgin forest of birch, alder, red and white pine. The Boundary Waters Canoe Area extends from here to Canada, a wilderness teeming with fish, beaver, and waterfowl. The **Chippewa National Forest** (661,161 acres) also includes myriad lakes. The Paul Bunyan legends suggest that these might be the hoofprints of a certain big blue ox, but then you must not believe everything you read. Bunyan is said to be modeled on French-Canadian lumberjack Paul Bunyan, a fighter in the anti-British Papineau Rebellion of 1837, and a famous *blagueur*.

The *voyageurs* were such men. These eighteenth-century French-Canadian settlers paddled their birch-bark canoes through the maze of islands and waterways, learning the lore of the Indians and fighting, cheating, and bragging. Travel to Kabetogama on Minnesota 122, north from U.S. Highway 53, and you arrive at the Kabetogama Lake Visitor Center of the **Voyageurs National Park** (219,400 acres), founded in 1975. To the northwest, Minnesota 11 leads from park headquarters at International Falls to Island View. Within the park the thoroughfares tend to be on water rather than on land – canoeing routes linked by portages. Four main lakes lie within the park area: Rainy, Kabetogama, Namakan, and Sand Point. In summer one can follow the 32 miles of hiking trails (accessible by boat), fish, or examine the natural history of the region, with adequate amounts of insect repellent. In winter you can snowmobile, follow the ice road on Rainy Lake, and ice-fish, or snowshoe and ski cross-country at Black Bay. Winters can be severe. The

Ancient glaciation has made the region now occupied by Minnesota's Voyageurs National Park into a pattern of lakes and islands. This has remained wilderness, the preserve of wolf, black bear, coyote, beaver, and loon. For humans there is the opportunity to canoe, ski cross-country, or hike the lakeland trails.

wild creatures of Voyageurs include the timber wolf, which hunts deer and moose.

Minnesota's southern border is with Iowa, a state typical of the Midwest in that it forms part of a vast, flat plain. Over 95 percent of its area is devoted to arable farming, a higher percentage than any other state. Many of the farms are still relatively small enterprises. To the east, the state is bordered by the Mississippi, to the west by the Missouri and Big Sioux rivers. The Des Moines River crosses Iowa, lending its name to the largest urban area and state capital. In the north of the state the **Union Slough National Wildlife Refuge** preserves 2,200 acres of prairie and marsh, attracting many species of migratory waterfowl. In the southwest, 7,823 acres of agricultural land and woods in the Missouri Valley are preserved at the **DeSoto National Wildlife Refuge**. Geese and duck flock to this site, and in summer visitors can enjoy swimming, boating, angling, and other pursuits. In northeastern Iowa the **Effigy Mounds National Monument** (1,475 acres) cares for the burial mounds of Amerindian peoples who inhabited the Mississippi bluffs long ago. Some mounds are shaped like birds and bears, others have simple geometric forms. The earliest remains belong to the "Red Ocher" culture of 2,500 years ago. Others belong to subsequent periods and cultures. Oneota Indians occupied the site about 600 years ago. Trails lead to views of the sites and of the majestic Mississippi. Approach Effigy Mounds on Iowa 76 north of Marquette.

To the west of Iowa, across the Missouri, lies Nebraska, another state which includes a large expanse of plains devoted to agriculture. Some 45 million acres are farmland, producing grain and root crops. The west of the state is ranching country: Nebraska supports about 7 million cattle.

Brooding earthen tumuli guard their ancient secrets at Effigy Mounds National Monument in Iowa. This was a burial site for various Indian cultures over a period of two millennia. Some of the burial sites are designed in the forms of animals.

Namakan Lake is one of the largest in Voyageurs, extending eastward to the Namakan River. Camping is possible on many of its tiny islands; its northern shores wash Ontario, Canada.

The terrain is dominated by the Platte River, its forks and tributaries. Following the North Platte westward, one comes to a wilder region, with rocky outcrops such as **Scotts Bluff National Monument**. This 2,988-acre site surrounds a slab of eroded rock which towers 800 feet (244 m) above the Great Plains. Named after Hiram Scott, a trapper of the pioneer days, Scotts Bluff became a famous landmark during the middle of the nineteenth century, when thousands of settlers headed west on the Oregon Trail. Their covered wagons were funneled through the Mitchell Pass, and the rutted tracks created by their passing can still be seen today. One can drive to the monument from U.S. Highway 26 at Scottsbluff; the main route westward, Interstate 80, now passes to the south. The visitor center is located on Nebraska 92.

A covered wagon is displayed as a poignant reminder that this was the route of the Oregon Trail, the historic route taken by pioneers traveling westward from 1841 onward. The great cliff in the background is Scotts Bluff, Nebraska, the famous landmark of those heady days. It towers above the North Platte valley.

Grazing land: shortgrass prairie of South Dakota. This was ideal hunting ground for the Indian tribes, in strong contrast to the barren badlands nearby.

The **Nebraska National Forest** occupies three sites in the center, north, and west of the state: Bessey, McKelvie, and Pine Ridge. Totaling 257,257 acres, the site includes plantations of pine amid prairie grass and sandhills. The **Oglala National Grassland**, named after a tribe of the Sioux, preserves typical prairie and badlands in the northwestern corner of the state. Nebraska has four areas set aside for the protection of its fauna: **Fort Niobrara** and **Valentine National Wildlife Refuges** are in the north, the former protecting prairie ruminants such as deer, bison, and Texas longhorns, the latter attracting birds such as bitterns and avocets. The **Rainwater Basin Wetlands Management District** in the south, and the **Crescent Lake National Wildlife Refuge** in the west, support large bird populations which include waterfowl and waders.

The **Agate Fossil Beds National Monument** is accessible via Nebraska 29, which links U.S. Highways 20 and 26. Here, among 2,700 acres of prairie and agate-bearing rocks on the Niobrara River, are the fossils of mammals such as rhinoceroses which roamed America around 20 million years ago, during the Miocene Epoch. A visitor center explains the importance of the region's paleontology.

To the north of the state line, South Dakota is typical of Great Plains terrain, from the fertile east to across the Missouri. In the west, the rolling prairies are interrupted by the rocky wilderness of the White River Badlands. Within the **Badlands National Park** are buttes, pyramids, cliffs, pinnacles, jagged teeth, and ridges sharp as tomahawks, surmounting rubble-strewn gullies. The story of these rocks begins some 80 million years ago, when sediment accrued on the floor of a shallow sea. About 65 million years ago the area was uplifted by movements in the earth's crust, along with the Rocky Mountains and the Black Hills. The exposed sedimentary shale was eroded, and then overlaid with riverine sediment, and, some 32 million years ago, with ash blown westward from volcanic eruptions. Today the record of the rocks is laid bare by erosion, and it is evidenced by the variously colored bands running along the cliff faces. Even more fascinating are the fossils which have been revealed. From these we can see with our own eyes the life

forms which flourished during the different prehistoric periods. Turtles, alligators, oreodonts, titanotheres and eohippi (ancestors of the horse) have been found. In more recent history, the prairies were grazed by more familiar herds, and Amerindian hunters scouted the badlands on hunting expeditions. The Arikara settled here, and finally the Sioux, dependent on the bison for their livelihood. White trappers penetrated the region, and then miners, soldiers, and settlers. All held the rocky crags in contempt, dismissing them as *mako sica, mauvaises terres à traverser*, or "badlands" – to Indians, French, or English-speakers, the lands were worthless. To later generations, however, the extraordinary fossils and savage scenery invested the badlands with a certain magic, and in response a national monument was formally established in 1939. A southern unit, homeland of the Oglala Sioux, was added in 1976, and in the same year the Sage Creek Wilderness Area was designated.

Today the full national park includes trails for hikers as well as scenic drives and overlooks. Bison and bighorn sheep have been reintroduced to the park area, and prairie rattlesnakes, cottontails, badgers, coyote, bats, prairie dogs, and pronghorns (familiarly referred to as antelope) complement the variety of wildlife. Bird lovers should look for the golden eagle, which winters here, for turkey vultures, rock doves, white-throated swifts, and cliff swallows. Botanists will note eastern red cedar, yellow willow, juniper, and cottonwood. The grasses of the open country include prairie junegrass, western wheatgrass, and side-oats grama. To approach the northeastern entrance of the park, take exit 131 from Interstate 90. This leads to the Cedar Pass Visitor Center and fine vistas of the badlands scenery. The south unit is approached on South Dakota 33 and 27 from the historic battlefield of Wounded Knee. The White River Visitor Center is open in summer only. Camping is available within the park, and accommodation in nearby towns. The whole park area is surrounded by the open prairie of the **Buffalo Gap National Grassland** (591,771 acres) and, to the south, the Pine Ridge Reservation.

Interstate 90 westward leads to Rapid City. To the south and west lie

Opposite: Wrinkled and furrowed, the bleak sprawl of South Dakota's badlands seems to belong to an alien planet. The Badlands National Park tells a fascinating story of geological upheaval and erosion, and never fails to amaze the eye.

The savage beauty of Badlands National Park, South Dakota. Striated ramparts of stone stretch mercilessly to the horizon. To the early pioneers these desolate regions were a major obstacle. To the modern tourist they are a fascinating spectacle.

the beautiful Black Hills of Dakota, rising to an elevation of 7,242 feet
(2,207 m) above sea level at Harney Peak. Prospectors staked their claims
here in the last century; today the range offers the visitor an intriguing
selection of attractions. The **Mount Rushmore National Memorial** lies
at the edge of the area, one of the best-known landmarks in the whole of
the U.S.A. Carved in its granite cliffs are gigantic heads of stone 465 feet
(142 m) high; George Washington, Thomas Jefferson, Abraham Lincoln,
and Theodore Roosevelt. Dynamited, jackhammered, and drilled from
solid rock between the years 1927 and 1941 they were conceived as a
shrine to democracy and executed by Idaho sculptor John Gutzon de la
Mothe Borglum. The monument is approached by U.S. Highway 16
from Rapid City, turning off southwest from Keystone.

From here South Dakota 87 leads southward through Custer State
Park to the **Wind Cave National Park**. It is joined by U.S. Highway 385
north of the visitor center. The limestone cavern is famed for its delicate
calcite crystal formations, and many of these can be viewed from a short
subterranean trail. Designated a national park as early as 1903, the
limestone rocks are surrounded by open prairie and stands of ponderosa

One of the most famous tourist attractions in the United States. South Dakota's Mount Rushmore has been tamed by drill and chisel and made into a shrine to the nation's ideals: George Washington, Thomas Jefferson, Theodore Roosevelt, and Abraham Lincoln stand captured in stone. The work took 14 years to complete.

Below: South Dakota's Wind Cave National Park lies to the south of the Custer State Park. Surrounding the caves, above ground, is open prairie, the home of pronghorns, prairie dogs, cottontail rabbits, and coyotes. Summers are hot and thundery on the prairie, and winters cold and snowy.

Below right: A bison rears it shaggy head to the sun. These fine creatures were hunted out in the last century, and only dogged conservation work has restored them to their natural habitat. The herd at Wind Cave National Park is some 350 strong. It was started off with just 14 zoo specimens, back in 1913.

pine. Bison, pronghorn, and prairie dog are natives of this habitat; bird life includes meadowlarks, chickadees, and sharp-tailed grouse. The park covers 28,056 acres. To the west of Custer State Park, U.S. Highway 16 leads to another geological treasure chest, **Jewel Cave National Monument**. An underground maze of limestone caves is entered here, and again the main attraction is the impressive formations of calcite crystal. There is a visitor center where information about the site can be obtained.

No camping is available at Jewel Cave, but the **Black Hills National Forest** affords many an opportunity for the camper. This forest surrounds the three above attractions, covering a total of 1,235,483 acres. The Black Hills contrast strongly with the vast flatlands, unfolding panoramas of ridges, crags, waterfalls, and lakes flanked by dark forests of pine. Recreation is centered upon lakes and reservoirs such as Pactola, Deerfield, and Sheridan. A visitor center at Pactola offers information about the many activities pursued in the national forest area, such as hiking, riding, boating, swimming, and winter sports.

Federally protected land is not limited to the southwest of the state. **Fort Pierre National Grassland** in central South Dakota, and **Grand River National Grassland** on the state's northern border, conserve wide expanses of prairie. From the Nebraska line across the Missouri and then to the northeast lies a chain of national wildlife refuges which offer a lifeline to the birds and other creatures of the river banks, lakeshores, and marshes. **Lacreek, Lake Andes, Madison Wetlands Management District, Waubay**, and **Sand Lake** are frequented by geese, swans, ducks, white pelicans, grebes, and hawks. North Dakota is a land of wide open spaces, cloven from northwest to southeast by the great waterway of the Missouri. To the east the land is peppered with small lakes, the result of glaciation in ancient times. These stretch northward to Canada; the friendship between the two North American nations is symbolized by the 2,300-acre International Peace Garden north of Dunseith on U.S. Highway 281.

The **Theodore Roosevelt National Park** (70,416 acres) is situated in the northwest of the state, west of Lake Sakakawea on the Little Missouri River. Theodore Roosevelt first visited the area in 1883, to hunt the fast disappearing herds of bison. He became involved in cattle breeding at the Maltese Cross and then the Elkhorn Ranch. It was here that Roosevelt came truly to appreciate the beauty of the wild, and the need for conservation. As president, he was to found the U.S. Forest Service and encourage the establishment of national parks and monuments. Today, the park that so fittingly bears his name forms two units. The North Unit is reached by U.S. Highway 85 between Watford City and Grassy Butte, and the South Unit borders Interstate 94 at Medora.

From the North Unit Visitor Center (open in summer only) a scenic driveway leads westward to and overlooks points of interest. The western section of this drive, to Oxbow Overlook, is closed in winter. Trails loop around the park: the Buckhorn, Achenbach, Caprock Coulee, and Upper Caprock Coulee. A short nature trail leads from the Squaw Creek campground. The South Unit has visitor centers at Painted Canyon (summer only) and at Medora. Trails in this sector include the Lone Tree Loop, the Petrified Forest Loop, Wind Canyon, Jones Creek, Talkington, Paddock Creek, and Ridgeline. A scenic drive, partly closed in winter, leads to viewing points and trailheads. A campground is located at Cottonwood. This is badlands territory, a savage, forbidding corrugation of striated rocks. Brigadier-General Alfred Sully, campaigning against the Sioux, referred to the Dakota badlands as "hell with the fires burnt out." He should have qualified this statement, for sometimes seams of coal ignite in the park, scorching the soil. Nevertheless, bleak as they may be, the beauty of the badlands is undeniable. The landscape, so barren in places, supports a surprising range of birds and mammals. Some of them inhabit the rocky ledges,

Tough going in the rugged badlands of North Dakota. The Theodore Roosevelt National Park is a world of barren rock; tenacious trees and shrubs have colonized clefts and hollows where there is sufficient water to sustain growth.

A harsh prospect: Fluted rock presents an impenetrable wall in the Theodore Roosevelt National Park, North Dakota. The fissured landscape of the badlands is the result of erosion by water and wind.

while others thrive in the grass and sagebrush or alongside the rivers. The magnificent golden eagle carries off rodents such as prairie dogs in its powerful talons. Mule deer and whitetailed deer are to be seen; bison have been reintroduced to their old stronghold, and longhorn cattle are also herded. Wildflowers delight the eye in the summer months. Riders and backpackers who wish to experience the fascinating wilderness

The cabin of former President Theodore Roosevelt from the Maltese Cross Ranch. It was in North Dakota that Roosevelt developed his love of the outdoors and his understanding of the need for the conservation of the American landscape. Today the cabin is sited next to the museum in the South Unit of the Theodore Roosevelt National Park.

firsthand must first obtain permits for backcountry camping.

Roosevelt is surrounded by the **Little Missouri National Grasslands,** and similar tracts of prairie are set apart at **Cedar River,** on the South Dakota line, and at two sites in the southeast of the state, which form the **Sheyenne National Grassland.** These areas include tall, mid, and short grasses, grazed by pronghorn and deer. Birds of the open plain include sharp-tailed grouse and the greater prairie chicken. Both of these galliformes are noted for their striking spring displays. Seeds, buds, and foliage provide food.

North Dakota's pattern of lakes, ponds, and rivers are an invaluable part of the North American ecosystem; their importance cannot be underestimated. From the **Crosby Wetland Management District** in the

northwest, a stopping-off point for migrating whooper and sandhill cranes, to the **Tewaukon National Wildlife Refuge** in the southeast of the state, a network of nature reserves sustains the delicate balance of nature. In the north are the national wildlife refuges of **Lostwood, Des Lacs, Upper Souris,** and **J. Clark Salyer. Devil Lake** is part of a wetland management district and together with **Lake Alice National Wildlife Refuge** provides a nesting ground for countless wildfowl. **Sully's Hill National Game Preserve,** nearby, is the home of ruminants: bison, whitetailed deer, and elk. In central North Dakota, **Lake Audubon, Lake Ilo, Arrowwood,** and **Long Lake** have been set aside, and the **Kulm** and **Valley City Wetland Management Districts** supervise many sites in the southeast.

The Southwest

Arizona, New Mexico, Oklahoma, Texas

The American Southwest might be said to start at the Sabine River and stretch westward to the Colorado, following the Mexican border along the Rio Grande. Its northern boundary might be described as extending from Lake of the Cherokees in the east to Lake Mead in the west. This vast area of 571,970 square miles covers four states: Oklahoma, Texas, New Mexico, and Arizona, famous for its Indian cultures. These states include several large conurbations, but much of the area is undeveloped, a rough and sometimes harsh expanse of open country, from the grassy plains and farmland of Oklahoma to the burning deserts of Arizona.

What is now Oklahoma – which means "home of the red man" in the Choctaw tongue – was bought from France under the terms of the Louisiana Purchase of 1803 and declared Indian Territory. Many Indian tribes, tragically displaced by white settlement and harassment, were resettled here; among them the Five Civilized Tribes from the Southeast, the Seminole, Creek, Choctaw, Chickasaw, and Cherokee, who were all granted lands in perpetuity. Treaties counted for little in the last century. Indian tenures were confiscated as a reprisal for their owners supporting the losing side in the years of Civil War, and thousands of white homesteaders poured into Oklahoma. In 1889 western Indian Territory was opened to settlement and Oklahoma Territory formed the following year. In 1907 Oklahoma became the 46th state of the Union with the fusion of Oklahoma Territory and Indian Territory. To the rest of the nation, Oklahoma came to symbolize the struggle of the small farmer to make a living. Three-fourths of modern Oklahoma is still farmland, but a great deal of its wealth derives from oil and other mineral resources.

To the south, Texas was Mexican territory until 1836 when settlers from the U.S.A. declared their independence. The world knows the story of the Alamo. After ten years of self-sufficiency, Texas joined the Union on December 29, 1845. This was, of course, cattle country, whence large herds were driven northward by cowboys to the markets of the Midwest. The twentieth century saw the exploitation of Texas' massive oil fields, and urbanization around San Antonio, Houston, Dallas, and Beaumont. Texas is famed internationally for its wealth and its ranching life style.

Westward across the Pecos, the ancient Indian homelands had been settled in places by the Spanish as early as 1598; they declared it the Kingdom of New Mexico. In 1771 it became part of Mexico proper, which achieved independence from Spain in 1821. However, in 1848, after the Mexican War, it passed under Union control, to become one of the United States in 1912. The Hispanic cultural influence has remained, however, and about 9 percent of the present population is Indian. Ranching, agriculture, and mineral resources, notably uranium, provide wealth. New Mexico was witness to the birth of a stark new era in 1945, when the desert northeast of Alamogordo saw the testing of Trinity, the world's first atomic bomb.

Arizona was also secured for the Union by the Mexican War of 1848 and it became a territory in 1863. The region was first explored by the Spanish four centuries ago, and to the last remained a stronghold of the proud Apache. Some 20 million acres remain Indian reservation land. Arizona was accepted as a state in 1912. The regional economy has been based on mining and ranching, and, increasingly, on tourism.

Oklahoma's rolling lowlands are drained by an extensive network of waterways. The Canadian River passes through the state from west to east. The waters of the Cimarron run southeast from the Kansas line, fringed by the dunes of Little Sahara before joining the great Arkansas River. The state's southern border is formed by the meandering Red River. In eastern Oklahoma the central plains yield to the wooded slopes and dammed lakes of the Arkansas River Valley, the Ozark Plateau, and the delightful scenery of the Ouachita Mountains. In the south are a series of low mountain ranges, the Wichitas and the Arbuckles. In the north are the Glass Mountains, eroded buttes which glisten with gypsum and selenite. Gypsum is also responsible for the geological spectacle of the Alabaster Caverns State Park, south of Camp Houston. The far northwest forms a long "panhandle" into the Great Plains, and culminates in Black Mesa (4,793 feet; 1,576 m).

The Oklahoman fauna is conserved in six national wildlife refuges. In the north, off U.S. Highway 64, the **Great Salt Plains National Wildlife Refuge** comprises 31,997 acres of scrub, woodland, river, and salt pan. Beavers and whitetailed deer are protected here, together with migrating waterfowl and whooping cranes. Watch for the scissor-tailed flycatcher (the male's pied tail-streamers are used in courtship display). The **Sequoyah, Tishomingo, Washita,** and **Optima** national wildlife refuges preserve a variety of habitats from riverine to grassland, which attract ducks, geese, white pelicans, bald and golden eagles.

The largest such protected area is the **Wichita Mountains National Wildlife Refuge** (39,020 acres). The last century saw the extermination of

Treasure Lake is one of many fine views to be seen in Oklahoma's Wichita Mountains National Wildlife Refuge. It lies to the southeast, on the edge of Charon's Garden Wilderness Area. A hiking trail leads from the Post Oak-Treasure Lake parking lot to the top of Elk Mountain.

the American bison, or buffalo, in the Wichita Mountains region. Reintroduced in 1907, today's herd of 625 beasts is testimony to the value of conservation. In the park you will also see Texas longhorns, whose wicked, curved horns serve as a reminder of the days of roundups and corrals. The grasslands are also home to rodents such as prairie dogs and rabbits. The forest supports elk, another species reintroduced after over-hunting. Bird life includes turkey and quail. Prairies, rocky outcrops, gorges, streams, lakes, and woods – the rugged scenery of the refuge is best viewed in summer or fall. The public use area lies in the east and south. Here you can enjoy fine views of the Wichitas from Mount Scott (2,479 feet; 756 m), fish for largemouth bass, sunfish, and channel catfish, or hike the Dog Run Hollow Trail. Backcountry camping, in the Charon's Garden Wilderness Area, is by permission only. The special use area, dedicated to large-scale conservation projects, is only accessible by officially guided tour. Camping is available within the refuge limits; the park is traversed by Oklahoma 49 and 115. The Quanah Parker Visitor Center offers information about the history and ecology of the Wichita Mountains.

In 1868 General George Custer ruthlessly massacred the inhabitants of a Cheyenne Indian settlement. Its chief was called Black Kettle, and today his name lives on in a 31,000-acre area of rolling prairie near the town of Cheyenne, Oklahoma. The **Black Kettle National Grasslands** have been set aside to preserve and propagate the species of grass indigenous to the region. The topography includes hills, lakes, and creeks, which attract a variety of wild creatures as well as anglers, boaters, and hikers. The wind-stirred grasses of the prairie serve as a fitting memorial to Custer's victims.

Oklahoma's Platt National Park is now incorporated in the **Chickasaw National Recreation Area.** This 9,500-acre site is divided into two separate units and may be reached by Oklahoma 7 and U.S. Highway 177 (off Interstate 35), and by Oklahoma 110. The region is celebrated for its freshwater and mineral springs, the latter containing iron, sulfur, and bromide. Trails loop around Travertine Creek from the nature center of the same name. To the southwest, the second unit surrounds the dammed waters of the Lake of the Arbuckles, and provides many recreational facilities.

Texas, a vast expanse of territory covering a variety of geographical areas and climatic zones, is the second largest state after Alaska. It lies on the Gulf of Mexico, and its great sweep of coastline extends northeast from the Rio Grande, shielded by a host of islands, spits, and lagoons. A subtropical coastal plain stretches inland, irrigated by a series of major rivers: the Nueces, San Antonio, Colorado, Brazos, San Jacinto, Trinity, Neches, and Sabine. The north and center of the state is fertile agricultural land, as is much of western Texas, which covers the lower extremity of the Great Plains. West of the Pecos River lie scattered mountain ranges and starkly beautiful canyonlands.

Some 177,000 acres of northern Texan prairie are conserved as national grasslands, the home of bobwhite quail, wild turkey, deer, bobcats, and coyotes. Forest habitats are centered around the **Big Thicket National Preserve**, 84,000 acres of densely wooded wilderness north of Beaumont. Its larger satellite forests are no less impressive: **Angelina, Davy Crockett, Sabine,** and **Sam Houston National Forests** consist of hardwoods, yaupon, shortleaf, longleaf, and loblolly pines, and harbor numerous wildflowers, including wild orchids.

The wildlife of Texas is as varied as the habitats it occupies. Over 215,000 acres are designated national wildlife refuges, and here sanctuary is afforded to bird species such as the endangered prairie chicken, ibis, egret, wood stork, roadrunner, and snowgoose; alligators, prairie dogs and mule deer are other creatures enjoying protection. The eastern end of the Mexican border has a unique subtropical vegetation, and three national wildlife refuges – **Rio Grande Valley, Santa Ana,** and (on the Gulf) **Laguna Atascosa** care for the exotic ecology of the region. Here

In 1553 a hurricane drove a whole Spanish fleet ashore on Padre Island, scattering a fortune in gold beneath the waves. Today, this national seashore offers a different kind of treasure: silver dunes, abundant birdlife, and swimming, fishing, and beachcombing for summer visitors.

An aerial view of the Aransas National Wildlife Refuge, Texas. The tidal marshes and ponds of the Blackjack Peninsula are inhabited by a huge variety of freshwater and saltwater birds. Aransas has become famous internationally as the wintering ground of the endangered whooping crane. The sandbanks and shallows are shaped by the stormy seas of the Gulf of Mexico.

The cougar or mountain lion is still to be found in Texas, a magnificent, lithe hunter. The inshore woodland of Aransas is hunted by bobcat, jaguarundi, and coyote as well as the cougar.

live the chachalaca, the Altamira oriole, and the leopard-like ocelot. Some of the most pioneering conservation work has been carried out at the Aransas National Wildlife Refuge, 54,829 acres on the Blackjack Peninsula, founded in 1937. Aransas Bay is a lagoon in the lee of the long sandbars of San Jose and Matagorde Islands. This is oil-producing country, and for once industrial and ecological interests seem to have established an amicable system of cooperation. The area is one of saltmarshes and freshwater ponds, yielding to grasslands and stands of live oak and red bay. This meeting of habitats has proved to be rich indeed. Here are javelina, alligators, cougar, coyote, jaguarundi. Roseate spoonbills, pelicans, and bittern are among 350 bird species; there are 21 kinds of snake, some venomous, nine species of lizard, seven species of turtle and terrapin, and 15 different amphibians. Aransas is best known for its whooping cranes. Once upon a time these elegant creatures flew over much of the United States. By 1948 only 15 survivors remained, at Aransas, and the hardships of their 2,500-mile migration to Canada suggested that their days were numbered. Scientists conferred, and research was carried out into their breeding patterns; their flight paths were carefully monitored across the continent. In the last decade young whooping cranes have been "fostered" onto flocks of sandhill cranes with some success, and separate breeding stocks built up in captivity. The gamble seems to be paying off, and the whooping crane has today become a symbol of conservation throughout America. Visitors are welcome at Aransas, which may be reached via Texas 2040 off 239/774 and Texas 35. Cranes are normally present between November and March.

South of Aransas and the city of Corpus Christi a seemingly endless spit of sand lies parallel to the coast, enclosing the Laguna Madre. Once the graveyard of Spanish galleons, the sandbar today forms the **Padre Island National Seashore**. The island is 113 miles long, and the federally protected land covers the 80 miles down to Port Manfield Channel, an area of 133,919 acres. An extension of Texas 358 from Corpus Christi takes one 10 miles onto the island, which is popular with anglers, swimmers, divers, surfers, and water-skiers. You will need a four-wheel drive vehicle to proceed toward Little and Big Shell Beaches, and before long you enter a lonely world of dunes, flotsam and jetsam, and the great expanse of sea and sky. Comb the shore for seashells, or watch the bird life of the Gulf: white pelicans flapping lazily across the horizon, greedy black skimmers, wading birds. The cattle which once grazed the island's coarse grasses are gone. Wild animals have colonized the barrier: gophers and jackrabbits, even coyote. Reptiles include the loggerhead turtle. Beware of the western diamondback rattlesnake, a predator of rodents which is extremely poisonous. Information for visitors is available at the Corpus Christi headquarters or at the Malaquite Visitor Center. Camping is available at Malaquite Beach, and it is possible to bivouac on the dunes.

West of the Edwards Plateau, Texas is a different land, an arid, often severe rockscape. The Chisos Mountains rise above a meander in the Rio Grande; it is from the latter that **Big Bend National Park** takes its name. The park, created in 1944, is made up of 740,118 acres of wild backcountry, approached by U.S. Highway 385, south from Marathon off U.S. Highway 90. A spring visit avoids the rigors of the summer heat and dust, and offers a rare chance to see wildflowers braving the rocky environment. The crags of the Chisos range are ancient and weathered. Sunset softens their contours: The red and buff sandstone cliffs glow warmly, and the plants – yucca, prickly pear, cactus, and creosote – cast long shadows. The thorny vegetation does little to deter the brown-and-white cactus wren, whose feather-bedded nest lies secure among the sharp spines. It feeds on seeds, insects, and small lizards. Rattlesnakes and ringnecks breed here, and some of the larger mammals: the javelina, coyote, cougar, and whitetailed deer. Park headquarters is at Panther Junction, and information is available at the Rio Grande, Castolon, and

Basin centers. Drive 47 miles from the Basin to the lonely splendor of Santa Elena Canyon, or, in the opposite direction, 25-mile-long Boquilla Canyon. To get the true feel of the old days along the border, take to horseback, or hike the 174 miles of park trails. Permits are necessary for boating and for backcountry camping. Always remember that the climate is extremely variable, that the going is sometimes tough, and that you will need to carry adequate water supplies. Camping is available within the park.

The highest point in Texas is Guadalupe Peak, at 8,751 feet (2,667 m).

The scorched valleys and rockfaces of Big Bend. The sandstone mountains were deposited millions of years ago as the sediment of an inland sea; they were raised high and then eroded into their present form.

Opposite: Big Bend's Santa Elena Canyon. It is best viewed in summer, shortly after dawn, when the morning is still cool, and the sun is illuminating its sheer cliffs and dark waters.

Sunset in Big Bend National Park, Texas, is time for the howling of the coyote. Agave, seen here, is typical of the tough vegetation which can survive the intense heat of summer and the barren rocky landscape along the Rio Grande.

The Guadalupe Mountains lie north of the Apache and Delaware ranges and run across the state line into New Mexico. In 1972, 76,293 acres of this chain were established as the **Guadalupe Mountains National Park**. The mountains rise from a shimmering plain. It is hard to believe that this wall of rock was ever buried beneath the sea – and yet the fossils remain to prove it, some 250 million years later. A horseshoe barrier reef once fringed this sea, forming a lagoon which later became a salt pan. The reef was eventually buried under sediment, and the rocks so formed later became uplifted during crustal turmoil. Erosive forces molded this new range, and revealed part of this fossilized reef. Canyons too were formed, and these have been colonized by a surprising number of trees and shrubs. Guadalupe wildlife includes wild turkey, raccoon, porcupine, and foxes, as well as very many birds and reptiles. The park's varied habitats include desert plain, conifer upland, and gulleys of broadleaves. The Guadalupe Trail and McKittrick Ridge are among 80 miles of trails for the hiker. Sites such as Williams Ranch and Frijole provide historical footnotes for the tourist. In the last century the Pinery was a staging post for the Butterfield Overland Mail Line, which took passengers westward through Apache territory. The climate in the mountains is capricious: hot and dry, or rent by summer thunderstorms. Backpackers should be well equipped, carry water at all times, and obtain backcountry passes. Guadalupe Mountains National Park lies on U.S. Highway 62/180, about 100 miles east of El Paso. The Frijole Information Center provides water and details of camping and activities. No other accommodation is available.

New Mexico is a land of deserts and mountains. The Rockies extend into the state from the north, with tall, snowcapped crests. Wheeler Peak, in the Sangre de Cristo range, reaches 13,160 feet (4,011 m). In the

south of the state, further mountain ranges run down to the state border: the Mogollon, Black, San Andres, Sacramento, and Guadalupe. Three river systems dominate New Mexico: the Rio Grande, the Pecos, and the Canadian. Eastern New Mexico forms part of the Great Plains region, while the northwest is part of the Colorado Plateau. Climate and vegetation are determined primarily by altitude.

Carlsbad Caverns National Park (established in 1930) is the result of the same geological processes as its southern neighbor, the Guadalupe Mountains National Park. It occupies a 46,755-acre site southwest of Carlsbad on U.S. Highway 62/180, and also includes a section of fossilized Permian reef. Here, however, seeping rainwater has over the ages created vast underground caves, which were later raised above the water table by movements of rock. These caves must be one of the most remarkable subterranean spectacles in the world. There are over 60 caverns in the park, and some of these are really vast: The Big Room covers some 14 acres. The dripping stalactites and stalagmites of the Hall of Giants, the Queen's Chamber or the Temple of the Sun fill one with awe. Artificial lighting transforms the shafts of limestone into a fantasia of exquisite beauty. Bat Cave is famous for another reason. Although you cannot visit the cave itself, you can see its inhabitants on summer evenings, as literally *millions* of bats stream forth from the mouth of the cave. A viewing area has been set aside for spectators, and the sight is truly amazing as they emerge from the underworld. By day the bats hang in the caves, asleep; by night they leave to hunt the small insects on which they depend. They winter to the south, in Mexico. Early explorers of the caves were delighted to find themselves knee-deep in bat-droppings. A questionable pleasure to some, you might say, but in fact this guano was to be commercially exploited for many years, being sold as fertilizer. Above ground, Carlsbad is typical Guadalupe country: crags and canyons rising from an arid plain, but supporting at its various altitudes a large range of plant and animal life. The latter includes gophers, raccoons, skunks, rattlesnakes, and more than 200 bird species. The park may be explored along the various nature trails; details are available from the visitor center. There is no campground inside the park, but accommodation is available nearby.

Parapets and crenelations of limestone in the extraordinary underground spectacle of Carlsbad Caverns, New Mexico. Over the ages a huge array of stalactites and stalagmites has been developed as water drips through the porous rock. The limestone belongs to the Permian period, dating back 250 million years.

The southwestern states have more than their fair share of geological marvels. Northwest of Carlsbad lies the **White Sands National Monument**, 144,420 acres of gypsum desert bordering the alkaline flats around Lake Lucero. It may be reached by U.S. Highway 70/82 between Alamogordo and Las Cruces. The area is one of dazzling, bleached dunes sweeping to the horizon. Some dunes are about 50 feet (15 m) high, and take their long-ribbed pattern from the prevailing southwesterly winds. The grains of sand have been created by the erosion of gypsum strata exposed by a crustal fault. The environment is a harsh one, to say the least, but such is the adaptabilityof nature that plants and animals have come to terms even with this. The hardy yuccas are to be found here, and desert mice and lizards have become white so that they are camouflaged against desert predators. For further information about this interesting site, call at the visitor center, and then follow the Heart of Sands Loop drive. Neither accommodation or camping is available at the monument itself.

Well to the west of this duneland, the **Gila National Forest** extends to the border with Arizona. Its 2,705,752 acres lie adjacent to Arizona's Apache-Sitgreaves National Forest, and consist of high desert and mountains, canyons and grassland, a lonely preserve of cactus, juniper, and pine. Gila (the first letter is aspirate) contains a wilderness area of the same name, the first to be officially designated as such, in 1924. Today the forest contains a second recognized wilderness area, namely that of Aldo Leopold. The high country, lakes, and rivers attract hikers, campers, and anglers, and drivers through the forest area are rewarded with fine views. Silver City provides an ideal base for exploration of the

A family of raccoons, one of America's more familiar nocturnal carnivores. Raccoons are among the wildlife to be found in the Carlsbad Caverns National Park.

127

area. In the last century this was mining country, and the heartland of the Apache nation. The great chief Geronimo (*c.* 1834–1909) rode these ranges and forded these streams. Other Amerindian people had also once settled this area, between the first and fourteenth centuries A.D. The first dwellers were Mogollon Indians, living in pithouses. Sometime after A.D. 1000, pueblo builders moved to caves in the cliff face. The ruins of these strongholds still line one canyon; some of the dwellings had as many as 40 rooms. The **Gila Cliff Dwellings National Monument**, a site of 533 acres, is open during the daytime, and can be reached by New Mexico 15, north from U.S. Highway 180 at Silver City.

Archeologists should also visit northern New Mexico. The **Bandelier National Monument** (32,737 acres) is situated due south of Los Alamos, north and west out of Santa Fe on New Mexico 4. These hauntingly beautiful canyonlands were occupied by Pueblo Indians between 800 and 500 years ago. Trails wind to the ruins of cliff homes. The mysteries of this historic settlement are explained at the visitor center. Camping near the monument is possible. To the northwest of Bandelier are the high snowlines of the **Santa Fe National Forest** (1,584,630 acres). Aspen and conifers blanket the slopes of the Jemez Mountains and the Sangre de Cristo to the east of Santa Fe, offering an intriguing maze of trails to the backpacker, striking vistas for the motorist, and a whole range of outdoor pursuits, from fishing to skiing. The **Carson National Forest** covers mountain ridges and valleys northward to the Colorado line.

The **Aztec Ruins National Monument**, 27 acres situated off U.S. Highway 550 in the northeast of New Mexico, is something of a misnomer. The ruins are pre-Columbian in origin, and were built not by Aztecs but by Indians of the Chaco Canyon culture sometime after the tenth century A.D. Later settlers adhered more to the Mesa Verde cultural pattern. The site was finally abandoned about 700 years ago, but pueblo ruins have survived to our own times. Northeastern New Mexico has evidence of human life from very much earlier times. Discoveries at

White Sands National Monument, New Mexico: Highlights and shadows form a striking pattern across the dunes. The wind sculpts the glistening grains of sand into long banks and ridges.

Folsom revealed the remains of prehistoric hunters and extinct animals. This is a volcanic area, and to the south of Folsom a gently sloping, almost perfectly conical mountain rises startlingly from the grassy plains. This is the **Capulin Mountain National Monument**, whose 775 acres are accessible via New Mexico 325, north from U.S. Highway 64/87. The statistics describe its topography: It is a cinder cone which rises to 8,182 feet (2,494 m) above sea level; from base to cone it is over 1,000 feet (305 m) high; the crater is 1,450 feet (442 m) across and 415 feet (127 m) at its deepest. A road spirals to the top; one trail descends into the dormant crater, while the other rings the rim, offering distant views of mountains and neighboring states. Piñon-juniper growth greens the dark mountainside, and wildflowers in season include lupin, golden pea, and verbena. Bird life on Capulin includes black-headed grosbeaks and other finches, bluebirds, and warblers. The visitor center, not far from the park entrance, offers interpretive programs about the environment and its geological past. Campgrounds are to be found at Capulin and Folsom, and overnight accommodation is available in Raton, Clayton, Des Moines, and, across the state line, in Trinidad.

Opposite: A reconstructed talus house or cliff dwelling in New Mexico's Bandelier National Monument. Visit Frijoles Canyon for an insight into the Pueblo culture of the period before Spanish rule. To the north of Frijoles, the Tsanakwi section offers panoramic views.

On the edge of the Gila Wilderness are pueblo dwellings of pre-Columbian Indians, built into the cliffs high above the West Fork of the Gila River. Their inhabitants would have farmed the mesa, growing squash, beans, and corn. Today, the Gila Cliff Dwellings National Monument may be visited by a one-mile self-guided trail.

The forests of central and southern New Mexico are managed by the **Cibola** and **Lincoln** national forests, while the open plains around Capulin come under the authority of the **Kiowa National Grassland**. Grassland habitats are conservation areas at **Maxwell** and **Las Vegas National Wildlife Refuges**, which protect hawks, eagles, prairie falcons, and rare peregrines. The **Bitter Creek** and **Bosque del Apache National Wildlife Refuges** both attract sandhill cranes, and the latter has become famous as the wintering ground for endangered whooping cranes fostered onto the sandhill species as part of the Aransas project.

Arizona occupies the southern part of the Colorado Plateau, and is bordered to the west by the Virgin Mountains and the great southern sweep of the Colorado River – canyon-carver extraordinary, dammed and controlled by humans in order to bring water to the parched deserts. Tributaries of the Colorado drain the high peaks of the plateau. The Gila River crosses the southern deserts above the Mexican border. Much of the state is an arid, harsh wilderness; nevertheless, it includes some of the nation's most spectacular landmarks and has a wild beauty all its own.

Arizona was not always the tract of baked rocks we know today. Some 200 million years ago, during the Late Triassic period, this was a wetland jungle, whose huge trees became buried in sediment and volcanic ash. Silica caused the organic matter of the trunks to become "petrified" or turned to stone. Millions of years passed by, and an inland sea that had flooded the area withdrew. Its sedimentary bed was heaved upward by a shift in the earth's curst, and soon the erosive forces of frost, sun, wind, and rain began to eat into the sandstone and shale. It was in this way that the buried forest first came to be exposed to the light of day. Today, the **Petrified Forest National Park** bears testimony to this incredible geological process. The trunks are preserved in every detail, tumbled and split into logs as if by some gigantic lumberjack. They glisten with white silica and are stained by colorful traces of iron and manganese dioxide. The park occupies 94,493 acres, and mineral traces in the striated

Opposite: Abandoned in the distant past, the walls of New Mexico's Aztec ruins are eloquent in their silence. This large archeological site is today a national monument.

These logs are in fact made of stone. Arizona's Petrified Forest contains whole trunks transformed by a strange geological process, whereby the wood fiber has become silicified. Mineral coloration and crystal-like formation make many samples very beautiful.

The Petrified Forest National Park and its Painted Desert are best explored in the spring or fall. The heaps of petrified timber and the colorful clay ridges have a strange beauty. Day hikers must prepare for desert conditions. In summer each walker will need about a gallon of water a day.

sedimentary rocks have created a badlands panorama of pink and brown: the Painted Desert, a beautiful but barren waste, inhabited by rattlesnakes, lizards, and rodents, and dotted with cactus and yucca. The national park is crossed by U.S. Highway 66 between Winslow and Gallup, New Mexico, and by U.S. Highway 180 west of St. John. The Painted Desert Visitor Center offers you an information service, and the story of the park is explained at the Rainbow Forest Museum. The Painted Desert is best viewed from Kachine Point, and Jasper Forest Overlook reveals the fossil timber in profusion. Do not miss Blue Mesa, Agate Bridge, Crystal Forest, the Long Logs, and Agate House. Hiking offers a more detailed examination of the area, but permits are required for wilderness and backcountry use. Water is essential for all such expeditions. Camping is not available in the park.

North of the Painted Desert are large areas of country set aside as reservation land of the Hopi and Navajo Indians. The center of Navajo territory is the **Canyon de Chelly National Monument**, 83,840 acres, first protected in 1931. De Chelly (normally pronounced "de Shay") is the name of a river which meanders westward from the Chuska Range to the Chinle Wash. It enters a stately canyon of sheer, weathered cliffs and is joined to the north by the Canyon del Muerto, which forks in turn to Black Rock Canyon. Three Turkey Canyon lies to the south. Spider Rock, a towering pinnacle of sandstone, towers 800 feet (244 m) from the floor of Canyon de Chelly, like some primitive rocket awaiting countdown. The Navajos fought Kit Carson across this wild landscape. Their traditional dwellings, log cabins known a "hogans", may still be seen today. Two thousand years ago the canyons were visited by nomadic Amerindian tribes, and from the fourth to the fourteenth centuries A.D. they were settled by the agriculturalists now referred to as Anasazi ("ancient ones"). Relics discovered have resulted in the earliest stage of their culture being referred to as "Basketmaker." Later stages

Spider Rock holds dizzying prospects at Arizona's Canyon de Chelly National Monument. Erosion by water, wind, and sun has created a landscape of towering pillars, rocky gorges, and tumbled scree.

The rugged cliffs of Canyon de Chelly have seen two thousand years of human settlement, and bitter wars between the Navajo and Spanish and American opponents. This national monument was established over 50 years ago.

saw the manufacture of pottery, and the building of pueblos and cliff dwellings. Anasazi ruins are to be seen at White House Ruin and Mummy Cave. Ancient wall drawings have been added to by Navajo artists, as at Antelope House and Standing Cow Ruin. The best way to view the monument is by driving along the north and south rims, which lead eastward from the visitor center to a series of observation points. The canyon floor may only be entered with official permission, and under favorable weather conditions. Camping is available at Cottonwood, and accommodation at Thunderbird Lodge. Approach from Chinle, off Arizona 63 (south from U.S. Highway 160, north from Interstate 40).

Sunset at Yaki Point, on the south rim of Arizona's Grand Canyon: The great cliffs mellow and plunge into shadow. This is one of the best-loved panoramas in the United States, and deservedly so. From Yaki Point one can hike down to the bottom of the canyon.

In the northwest of Arizona is the one canyon which defies the imagination. The **Grand Canyon National Park** (1,218,375 acres) is cleft by the world's largest terrestrial gorge. The mighty Colorado has excavated a deep chasm 217 miles long, 9 miles wide, and a mile from top to bottom. In Indian folklore, Grand Canyon marked the trail of a god named Tavwoats. The Spanish discovered Grand Canyon in 1540, and in 1869 one-armed explorer John Wesley Powell completed the arduous navigation of the Colorado, in the course of which two of his men were killed by hostile Indians. The area was made a national monument in 1908, and finally became a national park in 1919, after a long fight against commercial interests. In our own time the Grand Canyon has come to be regarded as one of the wonders of the world; it certainly provides its many visitors with an unforgettable experience. The buff-colored bastions of rock rise from the river's edge like the immense battlements of a crusader castle. The canyon floor receives a mere 7 inches (18 cm) of rainfall in a year and experiences desert conditions. From this roasting pan the cliffs rise to the south rim, clad with piñon-juniper vegetation, dusted by snow in winter and lashed by electric storms in late summer. The north rim is 1,000 feet (305 m) higher, reaching 9,000 feet (2,743 m) above sea level. Here, aspen yield to dark ranks of fir and spruce, and snowdrifts lie thick in winter months.

The north rim is approached by Arizona 67 south from Jacob Lake, and is open to the public in summer only. Follow the paved road to the ranger station and campground. Bright Angel Point reveals glorious views of brooding Deva, Brahma, and Zoroaster. The Uncle Jim Trail leads to a more northerly vantage point, and Transept Trail skirts the rim. The Cape Royal and Cliff Springs Trail take under an hour, while the Widforss and Ken Patrick trails take about five or six hours. The North Kaibab Trail leads down to the canyon floor, an exhilarating if sometimes exhausting experience. Roaring Springs is a day's walk, there and back, and water must be carried. Camping is available.

The south rim is open all year round, despite winter snow, and is more developed than the north. It is reached from Cameron by Arizona 64 and from Flagstaff by U.S. Highway 180. The visitor center offers an orientation program, and the Yavapai and Tusayan museums are further attractions. West Rim Drive and East Rim Drive offer amazing overlooks and panoramas. At sunset or dawn the rocks become infused with a golden glow. Walkers may choose a gentle stroll along the Rim Trail between Maricopa and Yavapai points. Part of this path is a self-guiding nature trail. The Bright Angel Trail takes one 8 miles down to the river, and the South Kaibab Trail 6 miles, descending from Yaki Point. The River Trail links the two along the canyon floor. Hikers should check out park regulations at the visitor center; permits will be required for backcountry camping. A mule ride is the traditional means of descent, and really adventurous visitors may emulate John Wesley Powell and navigate the turbulent Colorado by float or small boat. Camping and accommodation are available.

The Grand Canyon's north rim is the home of the rare, pine-dwelling Kaibab squirrel. The **Kaibab National Forest** (1,556,397 acres) flanks the national park, and is the home of mule deer and a herd of bison as well as the black, white, and gray squirrel. Camping is popular among the stands of spruce and fir. Central Arizona is taken up by further tracts of National Forest Service land, covering millions of acres: **Prescott, Coconino, Tonto,** and the western arm of the **Apache-Sitgreaves National Forest.** The forests include areas of rugged wilderness: Sycamore Canyon, Pine Mountain, Mazatzal, Sierra Ancha, and Superstition. The relief map reveals a land of mountains and canyons, of lakes and reservoirs. The plant life varies from fir, ponderosa pine, spruce, and aspen to chaparral scrub and cactus; the regional fauna includes mule deer, whitetailed deer, javelina, quail, and wild turkey.

Central Arizona is a focal point in the ancient history of the Southwest, with a remarkable number of archeological sites. High above the valley of the Verde is the **Tuzigoot National Monument,** a pre-Columbian settlement; to the southeast is the **Montezuma Castle National Monument,** which bears witness to the Sinagua civilization. The **Tonto National Monument,** with its cave buildings, was the home of Salado agriculturalists during the fourteenth century, and the **Casa Grande National Monument** in Coolidge is a Hohokam village of the same era. **Wupatki National Monument** lies east of U.S. Highway 89 and extends over 35,253 acres to the Little Colorado River. Wupatki ("tall house" in the Hopi language) is a pueblo which 900 years ago was raised to a height of three stories; it would have contained up to 100 rooms. Nearby is a stone amphitheater and an ancient ball court, as well

Boaters enjoy a peaceful backwater of the Colorado. The great gorge itself has been carved out over the ages by river flow. The erosive action has revealed two-billion-year-old rock at the bottom.

as the modern headquarters and visitor center. Here you can find out about the hundreds of ruins which make up the site, such as Citadel, Nalakihu, Lomaki, and Wukoki. The whole area shows evidence of contact between several pre-Columbian cultures.

A shattering event disrupted the Indians of central Arizona in A.D. 1064 or 1065: a volcanic eruption. An area of about 200 square miles was showered with debris, and it is believed that the volcanic activities continued over the next 200 years. No cloud is without its silver lining, however, and for a time the ash made the desert soil fertile, before winds once again made a dustbowl of the region. The evidence of the turmoil is all around: spatter cones, long tongues of lava, and ice caves formed in lava tubes. **Sunset Crater National Monument** covers 3,040 acres south of Wupatki on U.S. Highway 89. A loop road through **Coconino National Forest** land links the visitor centers of these two monuments. The cratered cinder cone rises to a height of 1,000 feet (305 m). This is 7,000 feet (2,134 m) above sea level, and the smooth reddish mound contrasts strangely with the snowy backdrop of the San Francisco Mountains. Fall is the best time to visit Sunset Crater; snow can prove a problem in winter.

In southeastern Arizona, the **Coronado National Forest**'s 1,780,196 acres stretch to the Mexican border and across the New Mexico state line. Its 12 sections include the wildernesses of Chiricahua, Galiuro, and Pusch Ridge, and many famous scenic areas such as the Madera Canyon in the Santa Rita Mountains. The latter section of the forest is much visited by ornithologists; over 200 species of birds have been recorded, and the area also supports mammals such as deer, javelina, and coatimundi, a relative of the raccoon. The forest habitats vary from

Salado Indian ruins in the Tonto National Monument, Arizona. Seven centuries ago these people built their cave dwellings in the inhospitable Upper Sonoran Desert. They farmed and hunted, wove textiles and made pottery.

139

desert scrub to mountain, and offer a wide range of recreational possibilities, such as skiing, fishing, boating, hiking the many trails, or riding the bridlepaths. Important mountain ranges within the Coronado include the Pinalemos (Mount Graham has an elevation of 10,713 feet; 3,265 m); the Galiuro and the Santa Catalinas, northwest of the city of Tucson. Mount Lemmon (9,157 feet; 2,791 m) overlooks the Santa Cruz Valley. Chiricahua Peak rises to 9,795 feet (2,986 m) and towers above the **Chiricahua National Monument**. Approached by U.S. Highway 666 and Arizona 181, this is another region shaped by volcanic activity. Subsequent erosion has tortured the rock into fantastic pinnacles and columns. This whole area is redolent of the days of gun law. The mountains were the domain of the great Apache chief Cochise, whose rocky stronghold may still be seen to the south of Mount Glenn, west of U.S. Highway 666. Beyond the Dragoon Range lies the historic frontier town of Tombstone.

The **Saguaro National Monument**, established in 1933, is a short drive out of Tucson. Its 83,576 acres are divided into two sections, the Tucson Mountain Unit and the Rincon Mountain Unit. The former lies to the west of Interstate 10 on Kinney Road; the latter lies to the east of the city, and is approached via the Old Spanish Trail off Houghton Road. Both units contain great stands of saguaro and scrub typical of the Sonoran Desert; the Rincon Unit also includes coniferous, high-mountain vegetation. Mica Mountain reaches a height of 8,666 feet (2,641 m), and as one ascends from the desert floor one passes through stands of oak, ponderosa pine, and finally cool, shady firs. In both units however, it is the saguaro which captures the imagination. The largest cactus in the world, its spiny fingers and parallel branches point to heights of over 50 feet (15 m) and symbolize more than any other plant the unique beauty of the Sonoran Desert. These giants grow very slowly, taking a human lifespan to reach their maximum height, and they can live

Clouds mass above Sunset Crater National Monument, Arizona. This eerie landscape was created by volcanic eruptions about nine centuries ago.

Dramatic desert landscape in the Runcorn Mountain Unit of Saguaro. Many creatures and plants have adapted to life in this cruel environment.

for 200 years or more. With its pulpy stems and tough coat, the saguaro is designed to wring every last drop of moisture from a hostile environment; its shallow roots spread over a large area to maximize intake of rain during the winter and summer season. The flowers are cream-colored, and the crimson fruit contains black seeds. The Gila woodpecker, a fawn-colored omnivore with a red cap and black-and-white tail feathers, drills out nesting holes in the saguaro; when these are abandoned they are often occupied by other species, such as the purple martin, the ash-throated flycatcher, the house finch, and the elf owl (the smallest of its kind). The giant cactus also provides food for mammals – the javelina, coyote, and mule deer will feed on the fruit. The desert may be a harsh environment, but it does support myriad life forms, from tortoises to coachwhip snakes, from bats to ground squirrels. Mountain creatures include coatimundis, chipmunks, Mexican juncos, and jays.

The Ricon Mountain Unit of the monument contains a scenic drive; opportunities abound for studying the botany of the park as well as for viewing the expanses of desert and mountain scenery. Hikers can attempt the Tanque Verde Ridge Trail which leads eastward from the visitor center to the peaks; if you wish to camp overnight you must first obtain a backcountry permit. The Tucson Mountain Unit has an information center on the Kinney Road. This leads to Bajada Loop, Golden Gate Road, and trailheads. Neither section of Saguaro National Monument has accommodation or campgrounds, but then Tucson is very close to the park. Adjacent to the Tucson Mountains Unit is the Arizona-Sonora Desert Museum.

The **Organ Pipe Cactus National Monument** lies on the Mexican border about 115 miles due west of Saguaro and southeast of the Growler Mountains. It is situated on Arizona 85, north of Lukeville and south of the enigmatically named town of Why. Its 330,600 acres take in the Bates and Puerto Blanco ranges, the Quitobaquita and Cipriano hills, and the valleys of Sonoyta and the Ajo. In the east, Mount Ajo is 4,808 feet (1,466 m) above sea level. From the visitor center, 17 miles south of the entrance to the monument, graded dirt roads lead east and west. The Mexican border is followed by the Puerto Blanco Drive and the Camino de Dos Republicas. A spur of the former leads to the Senita Basin. The prickly organ pipe cactus, which in summer bears attractive pink flowers, is here in its element. Other cactus species include cholla, saguaro, prickly pear, and senita. Scientists are particularly fascinated by this region as it represents a meeting place of three different kinds of desert vegetation zone: the Upland Arizona Succulent Desert, the Central Gulf phase of the Sonoran Desert, and the California Microphyll Desert. So unique is this habitat that in 1976 the monument was declared by UNESCO to be an "international biosphere reserve." The region is best visited in winter, for the summer temperature can soar to 105°F (41°C). Many wild creatures have adapted to these conditions: They hunt by night or at twilight and hide away during the heat of the day. The park's fauna includes kangaroo rats, bobcats, kit foxes, coyote, desert tortoise, and Gambel's quail. The frenetic roadrunner seeks tirelessly after lizards, scorpions, rattlesnakes, and seeds and fruit. The park scenery is often beautiful, a wilderness of tumbled rocks, shrubs, and dry, coarse grasses, seasonally blanketed with wildflowers. This was bandit country in the old days, braved by ranchers and miners. Like the old timers, today's visitors should have a healthy respect for desert temperatures and terrain. There are short trails for the hiker and the naturalist, but permits are

Sonoran vegetation in the Organ Pipe Cactus National Monument: white brittle bush, chain cholla, saguaro, and organ pipe cactus interspersed with Palo Verde trees.

Organ pipe cactus is aptly named, its tall stems rising in clusters. In summer it has pink blooms, and provides a splash of color in the wilderness. The Organ Pipe Cactus National Monument in Arizona is of international ecological importance.

required for climbing or spending the night backcountry. Camping is available.

In southwestern Arizona, over 1½ million acres of land come under federal protection because of the wildlife to be found there. The **Cabeza Prieta National Wildlife Refuge** is the largest, lying immediately to the west of the Organ Pipe Cactus National Monument. In these mountains and deserts pronghorns and bighorn sheep are protected. To the north, the **Kofa National Wildlife Refuge** also consists of bighorn country, surrounding Castle Dome Peak. Three more national wildlife refuges lie on the California border: **Imperial**, **Cibola**, and **Havasu**. These areas include rather wetter habitats, thanks to the Colorado River, and are the haunt of herons, egrets, and the rare Yuma clapper rail.

The Mountain States

Colorado, Idaho, Montana, Utah, Wyoming

The backbone of North America is known as the Continental Divide: A long sweep of ranges form a mountain wall from Canada to New Mexico. To the east of the divide, the Great Plains form a huge watershed, draining into the mighty Mississippi-Missouri and other river systems. To the west are the arid lands of the Basin region, high plateaux, series of barrier ranges, and the great river systems of the western watershed, the Columbia and the Colorado. The dividing ranges are known collectively as the Rocky Mountains, a name which resounds through the annals of the West. The Mountain States have an individual character, and their peoples have fought hard to carve out a living from this rugged landscape.

The first settlers were Amerindian, and over the ages many different civilizations came and went; the Mesa Verde agriculturalists of Colorado, hunters and gatherers, pueblo-builders. It is the Indian nations of the nineteenth century whose resistance to the white settlers has become famous. General George Custer was defeated by Sioux and Cheyenne in Montana's Little Big Horn Valley in 1876. Utah was settled by members of Brigham Young's Mormon sect in 1847. The territory was under Mexican jurisdiction until 1848, when it passed to the United States. Despite conflict between the Mormons and the federal administration, Utah was admitted as a state in 1896. Part of Colorado was formerly under French rule, passing to the U.S.A. with the Louisiana Purchase of 1803. The remainder was yielded by Mexico in 1848, to become a full state 28 years later. The lofty peaks of Colorado concealed gold, silver, and copper, tales of which brought many pioneers westward from the eastern seaboard. Wyoming, cowboy country par excellence, was opened up by Oregon Trail overlanders in the 1840s, and later by the engineers of the Union Pacific Railroad. The territory became a state in 1890. Montana had joined the Union in the previous year, 86 years after the purchase of its lands from France. Montana's forests and open country attracted lumber outfits and farmers, while the considerable mineral resources also brought wealth to the region. Idaho became a state in 1890, also having been settled by lumberjacks, miners, and ranchers.

Today, the natural resources of the mountain states still support forestry, mining, and agriculture, and these in turn have given birth to a range of processing industries. Interstate highways now ease one's way past the canyons and buttes which obstructed the covered wagons of the last century, and yet despite this the Old West is never far away. Rodeos still pack in enthusiastic crowds, and the names along the highway evoke old memories: Roundup, Buffalo, Laramie, Cheyenne, Medicine Bow, Steamboat Springs, Durango. Drive through Wyoming by moonlight and the lonely, shadowy folds of the hills seem to be peopled by the ghosts of braves and medicine men, of gunfighters and cavalry braggarts. The clear air and snowy mountains of the Wild West are invigorating and magnificent, but the region is often eerie too. This is a fascinating land of bizarre rock formations and caves, of infinite pale salt flats which seem as

Perfect natural symmetry reflected in still waters. Known to Navajo as Nonnezoshi or "petrified rainbow," Rainbow Bridge still forms a high arc over this desert creek. Its pink rock is streaked with iron oxide. The bridge is accessible by a desert hike via the abandoned Rainbow Lodge, and by horseback or foot via Navajo Mountain Trading Post. Permits are required, and proper planning essential. Most visitors arrive by boat from Lake Powell.

if they should be the setting for some apocalyptic dream.

The Mountain States offer some of the most enjoyable touring in the U.S.A. presenting marvelous opportunities for motorists and backpackers alike. The west still has vast areas of wilderness and forest, and many of these are under federal protection in national parks. Many of the region's more extraordinary natural features are preserved as national monuments, and the **Continental Divide National Scenic Trail** links many of the most scenic parts. It is planned to extend this epic path until it joins Canada with Mexico, a distance of over 3,000 miles.

Utah has over 7 million acres set aside for administration by the U.S. Forest Service. These include the tortuous canyonlands of the southern **Dixie National Forest**, the aspens, spruce, and pine of the **Fishlake National Forest**, and **Manti-La Sal's** scattered enclaves of grassland, plateau, and piñon-juniper vegetation. The **Wasatch National Forest** is a short drive from Salt Lake City, offering excursions into a wilderness of exceptional beauty. The mountain streams are flush with trout, and high lakes reflect the craggy peaks of the Wasatch Mountains. Hikers will see mule deer and elk, and moose inhabit the forested valleys. In **Uinta National Forest** conifers such as Douglas fir mix with broadleaves such as oak and maple. In spring and fall stands of the latter provide a colorful backdrop to the canyonlands around Mount Timpanogos. Uinta is commercially operated timber country; many forests in this often parched landscape serve another purpose – as collectors of life-giving rains.

The forests and mountains of Utah are the habitat of a variety of mammals, and many species of migratory bird flock to the state's wetland areas. The saltmarshes of the **Bear River Migratory Bird Refuge** attract waterfowl and waders in profusion. To the southeast, the **Ouray National Wildlife Refuge** provides a crucial resting place for travel-weary sandhill cranes, and a hunting ground for eagles. To the southwest the **Fish Springs National Wildlife Refuge** offers a chance to see swans, egrets, and flocks of duck. The **Pariette Wetlands** provide another haven for wildlife, and the **Henry Mountains Buffalo Herd** grazes the beautiful highlands of southeastern Utah. Two centuries ago, herds of bison are thought to have numbered some 60 million. Systematic slaughter by white settlers destroyed these magnificent herds and brought the bison to the point of extinction. The moral is clear to modern conservationists. The above two conservation areas are in the care of the Bureau of Land Management. It also looks after sites of archeological or historical interest such as the Grand Gulch Primitive Area, and areas of natural beauty such as Labyrinth Canyon or the lunar landscape of Bonneville Salt Flats, one of Utah's most distictive natural features.

Utah's **Rainbow Bridge National Monument** rises from 160 acres of rough, stony country north of the Arizona state line. The rock formation does resemble a petrified rainbow, its rosy-colored sandstone forming the world's largest natural arch. It rises to a height of 290 feet (88 m) and spans 275 feet (84 m). The monument was held in awe by Hopi and Navajo Indians, and lies in arduous backcountry under a baking sun. It may be reached by horseback or on foot, or by boat. Details of access may be obtained from the **Glen Canyon National Recreation Area.** Here the dammed waters of the Colorado River spill into the ragged confines of Lake Powell. Over a million acres of rock-strewn territory include the wonderful Escalante Canyon. Wind, water, sun, and dust are powerful eroding forces, and they have worn down, cracked, and molded many of the rocks in southeastern Utah. The **Natural Bridges National Monument** is carved from tawny sandstone. Three great arches, Owachomo, Kachima, and Sipapu, have been created by erosion. The 7,799-acre site is best visited in winter. Access is via a spur of Utah 95, which may be reached from Utah 263, Utah 261 north from Mexican Hat, or U.S. Highway 163 south of Blanding.

Northeast of the Glen Canyon area the Green River merges with the

mighty Colorado. Upstream from their confluence the two powerful outflows from the snowy peaks of the Rockies have created a surreal landscape from the red sandstone of the Colorado Plateau. Covering 337,570 acres, the **Canyonlands National Park** is reached by turn-offs from U.S. Highway 163 south from Interstate 70. The nearest town is Moab, where the park headquarters is situated. The park is best explored by four-wheel drive vehicles, which are available for hire. Parts of the park are accessible by regular vehicles. Camping is limited, and permits are required backcountry. Canyonlands is one of the strangest places on earth. The park is a desolate, barren expanse of layered rocks. They lie in great slabs and contorted shapes, in curving basins, plunging canyons, and flat-topped mesas. Tall monoliths stand like the ruined columns of a giant's temple. Between the two rivers the Island in the Sky area affords commanding views of the park and distant mountains from Grand View Point. The tough backcountry of the Maze deters most visitors, but offers further rocky panoramas. Fall or spring are the best times to visit Canyonlands, for it has a desert climate with extreme temperature ranges. Sparse vegetation is browsed by mule deer and bighorn, and

Sipapu is a beautiful example of Utah's famous natural bridges. It stands 220 feet (67 m) high, and has a span of 268 feet (82 m). There are three such bridges, eroded from desert sandstone, in the national monument.

A meander through the rocky steps of the Colorado Plateau at Dead Horse Point, Utah. The geological strata are clearly revealed in this textbook study of erosion.

Overleaf: Canyonlands National Park, Utah, glimpsed through Grand View Arch. Erosive forces have quarried the rock into fractured terraces, pits, and upended slabs and columns. The Colorado River flows across the park.

predators include coyotes, cougar, and foxes. These barren lands were occupied by humans in ancient times. Wall drawings in Horseshoe Canyon, in the far west of the park, show that Amerindian peoples were living here more than ten centuries ago. Later visitors included rustlers and bandits, cattle herders and explorers, and patriarchal Mormons. Today's visitors come to marvel at nature's wonders, to tackle strenuous hikes, or to float downstream to Cataract Canyon.

Upstream from Moab, **Arches National Park** extends northward from the bank of the Colorado River. Its 73,379 acres are linked with Canyonlands by Utah 279, which links with U.S. Highway 163 near Moab. Here again the landscape has been contorted by erosion, creating a wilderness of sandstone columns, balanced rocks, and caves. Landscape

Arch is 291 feet (89 m), the longest-spanned natural arch in the world. Technically, this kind of arch differs from a natural bridge in that it is created by the effects of erosion on rocks that have become warped and segmented. Bridges on the other hand are bored through rock when a stream decides to take a short cut across a meander. Over 80 arches have lent the national park its name: Delicate Arch is one of the park's most elegant examples of nature's architectural skills. Roads lead to many of the park's most interesting features, and hikers may follow fascinating trails. Camping is available, but permits are required for backcountry, and in the considerable heat ample water supplies should be carried at all times.

Northeast of the Glen Canyon National Recreation Area, **Capitol**

Double Arch typifies the extraordinary rock formations to be found within Arches National Park, Utah: It sprawls over the barren wasteland like the roots of a gigantic tree. As the shadows deepen, the rock seems to take on a life of its own.

Opposite: Delicate Arch has all the poise and balance of a work of art, sculpted by water and appearing to defy gravity. Spring and fall are the best time for a visit to Arches National Park.

Reef National Park stretches northward from Halls Creek. With an area of 241,904 acres, the park is crossed by the course of the Fremont River on its journey southeast from Mount Terrell. The Colorado Plateau is here folded into a massive rampart of rock to form the Waterpocket Fold. This remarkable geological feature was thrust up by the same crustal turmoil that created the Rockies. For 100 miles the rust-colored cliffs rise from a jumble of scree, carved and weathered to form domes and clefts and pedestals of sandstone. Capitol Dome surmounts this long "reef"; below its bare crags the river valley supports willow and water-loving shrubs. The arid uplands are typical piñon-juniper zones. The visitor center at Fruita is a former Mormon settlement. Here you can find out about the reptiles and desert creatures which inhabit the park, about the Indian peoples whose ancient carvings still decorate the rocks, and about the hiking trails around Capitol Reef. Permits are required backcountry, and backpackers are reminded to carry adequate water supplies at all times. The desert climate is an adversary to be respected.

The coyote, America's wolf-like wild dog, hunts the Canyonlands by night. It is a stealthy creature, about 42 inches (1.07 m) in length, and hunts rodents and small game. It is more often heard than seen.

Camping is available within the park, but neighboring towns outside the park perimeter also offer accommodation. A drive within the park reveals fascinating rocky vistas; trips can also be arranged using four-wheel drive vehicles. Capitol Reef National Park lies on Utah 24 between Loa and Hanksville, off Interstate 70.

Traveling south from Salina on U.S. Highway 89 (off Interstates 15 and 70), turn east 6 miles after Panguitch on Utah 12 to Ruby's Farm; alternatively drive west from Boulder and Escalante on Utah 12. This

The Castle, an aptly named rock formation atop Capitol Reef in southern Utah. Capitol Reef is the name given to a section of the Waterpocket Fold. This "monocline" or single geological fold on the Colorado Plateau stretches from Thousand Lake Mountain towards Lake Powell. The area was declared a national monument in 1937, and a national park in 1971.

will lead you to another geological extravaganza: **Bryce Canyon National Park** (35,835 acres). Founded in 1928 and named after pioneer Ebenezer Bryce, the park lies between Sevier's East Fork and the Paria River. At this point the Paunsaugunt Plateau, 8,000 feet (2450 m) above sea level, is rimmed by a deep escarpment known as the Pink Cliffs. In geological terms these are relatively recent rock formations, consisting primarily of shale and limestone. Their colors are truly fantastic: pink, purple, orange, scarlet, ocher, white, and buff. Even more curious are the shapes that these sedimentary rocks have been sculpted into by erosion. Huge amphitheaters of rock present a never-ending spectacle; delicate stone towers and pilasters rise up in rococo excess, reminding

one of great chess pieces or bowling pins waiting to be tumbled down. Many of these rocks have been given fanciful names. The skyline is fringed by scattered conifers. The park contains mule deer, porcupines, squirrels, and badgers, and in summer splashes of color are created by wildflowers. Trails and bridle paths meander between the rocks, the most famous trail being the Navajo Loop. Panoramic views of the formations may be seen from Fairyland View, Sunset Point, Inspiration Point, Paria View, and Bryce Point. In winter the snows close in and the park may be explored on skis or snowshoes. Permission must be obtained for backcountry treks and for winter camping. Summer camping is available for periods of up to two weeks.

Overleaf: Bryce Canyon is not in fact a true canyon, but a natural amphitheater in the Pink Cliffs of the Wasatch Formation. The Paiute Indians had a word for it: Unka-timpe-wa-wince-pokitch, or "red rocks standing like men in a bowl-shaped canyon." Rain, snow, and ice have created this extraordinary spectacle, fashioning tall pillars of rock in profusion.

Sedimentary rocks are often very porous and easily carved and shaped by water, forming canyons and other bizarre formations. Hickman Bridge is a typical example, located in Capitol Reef National Park, Utah.

The traditional way of exploring the canyons, strung out along the trail. One can take a two-hour ride to Bryce Canyon floor, or a half-day round tour, and experience the same sense of elation as early pioneers such as Ebenezer Bryce.

No visit to southern Utah is complete without a visit to Bryce Canyon's larger neighbor, the **Zion National Park** (147,035 acres). The park takes its name from Zion Canyon, a deep fissure incised in soft plateau rock by the Virgin River, a powerful tributary of the Colorado. It was the Mormon Brigham Young who called the canyon Zion; many of the park's geological features bear ecclesiastical names, and appropriately enough, for the mesas and buttes and fluted rockfaces and fractured canyons resemble nothing so much as the nave, transepts, spires, and gargoyles of some immense Gothic cathedral. Eroded sandstone and shale formations reveal a variety of hues: brown, white, red, pink, purple, and fawn. In winter the cliffs are overlaid with snow; during the thaw one can see why the Indian name for Zion was *Mukuntuweap*, the "land of springs." Summer storms can also create flash floods. The valley floor and damp canyon grottoes provide oases in the barren environment which attract wildlife. Here are cottonwoods and elders; piñon and juniper cling to the mid-slopes, yielding to ponderosa pine and firs. Visit Zion National Park in spring, summer, or fall. Camping is available inside the park or in nearby towns. Hikers and

A winter storm blankets Zion National Park with heavy snow, lending an air of mystery to the high cliffs of Navajo sandstone. Zion is one of Utah's most impressive sights.

The Queen's Garden Trail at Bryce Canyon is an easy-going stretch with some of the best views in the national park. It starts from Sunrise Point: One can spend an hour or two wandering through the bristlecone pines and wondering what each pillar reminds one of. For really fine views and more strenuous exercise one can combine this hike with the Navajo Trail.

horse riders will find challenging trails, and motorists too can enjoy panoramic overlooks. Zion is situated south of Cedar City off Interstate 15. Turn onto Utah 17 and 15, which lead to park headquarters at Springdale. For the park's eastern approach, turn onto Utah 15 from U.S. Highway 89 at Mount Carmel Junction.

Southern Utah does not have the monopoly of geological marvels. Mount Timpanogos, 11,750 feet (3,580 m) above sea level, rises in the Wasatch Range, south of Salt Lake City. Approach via the Uinta National Forest. Take Utah 80 (joined from Interstate 15 between the state capital and Orem), and you come to the **Timpanogos Cave**

National Monument. This 250-acre site, open during the summer months, comprises three limestone caves in which seeping water has encouraged calcareous formations known as helictites. The caves glisten in a variety of colors – shades of green, pink, and yellow.

If any state epitomizes the great outdoors, it has to be Colorado, which straddles many of the great ranges which together make up the high Rockies: Medicine Bow, Park, Front, Gore, Sawatch, and Elk. In the south of the state the high chains of San Juan and Sangre de Cristo sprawl southward into New Mexico. The wildlife of this unspoiled backcountry includes pronghorn antelopes and mule deer, bighorn sheep

A study in erosion. F.S. Dellenbaugh, topographer for the renowned nineteenth-century explorer John Wesley Powell, enthused: "We are impressed with the marvelous beauty of outline, the infinite complication of these titanic buttes..." Modern visitors to Zion are sure to echo his sentiments.

Zion National Park, Utah. The bluffs of Navajo sandstone are weathered and eroded, forming a mellow backdrop to scattered trees.

(the official state animal of Colorado), elk, feral horses, black bears and grizzlies, coyotes, foxes, eagles, hawks, migrating waterfowl, and cranes. Birds come under special protection in the south at the **Alamosa** and **Monte Vista** national wildlife refuges, in the north at the **Arapaho National Wildlife Refuge,** and also in the far northwest at **Browns Park National Wildlife Refuge**.

The Continental Divide National Scenic Trail crosses many of the state's federal forests. Over 14 million acres of the state come under this category, and include some of the finest scenery in the land. In the north the **Routt National Forest** takes in the Mount Zirkel Wilderness; the **Roosevelt National Forest** covers part of the eastern watershed of the Rockies; the **Arapaho** and **White River** national forests surround lofty, snow-capped summits and alpine lakes. The **Grand Mesa-Uncompahgre National Forest** occupies the high tablelands and mountainsides of southwestern Colorado. It was Theodore Roosevelt who described Uncompahgre as "the incomparable valley with the unpronounceable name." To the east lie the forests of the **Gunnison, San Isabel,** and **Pike.** In the south are the canyons and waterfalls of the **San Juan National Forest** and the gold-bearing mountains of the **Rio Grande National Forest**. Away from the high country of the Continental Divide, the prairie lands offer a habitat every bit as interesting in their own way; the **Pawnee National Grasslands** are in the northeast of the state, while the **Comanche National Grasslands** are in the far southeast.

Lying on the Utah-Colorado state line is a national monument which takes the visitor back in time over 145 million years. During this period of prehistory the region was roamed by some of the strangest animals the world has ever seen: the dinosaurs. This was the home of stegosaurus, a dragonlike creature with huge plates rising from its back; apatosaurus, a long-necked vegetarian colossus; and allosaurus, a vicious predator with powerful jaws and teeth. The bones of these beasts became buried and preserved in sandy river sediment. Over the ages, inundation by sea and geological upheavals petrified the remains of the dinosaurs and other life forms, compacted sediment into hard rock, and thrust them upward. The sandstone began to erode, revealing the fossilized forms of the dinosaurs. They were discovered by paleontologist Earl Douglass in 1909. The **Dinosaur National Monument** was founded six years later. It was to yield up the fossils of 14 species of dinosaur as well as turtles and crocodiles. Today its 211,141 acres are covered in sagebrush and scrub rather than prehistoric conifers and gymnosperms, and its wildlife – plump sage grouse and darting tree lizards – are on rather a smaller scale than the monsters of the past. The dry, rocky terrain is split by deep canyons, through which rushes the white water of the Yampa and Green rivers. Monument headquarters are on U.S. Highway 40, 2 miles east of Dinosaur, Colorado; drive north from here on Harper's Corner Scenic Drive to a series of canyon overlook points. The place to see the dinosaurs is the Dinosaur Quarry Visitor Center on Utah 149 north from Jensen.

Northwest of Boulder, the 266,957 acres of the **Rocky Mountain National Park** may be reached via U.S. Highway 34 eastward (for the

Fossilized dinosaur bones protrude from the bed of rock at the Dinosaur National Monument (Utah and Colorado). The Dinosaur Quarry Visitor Center offers an intriguing insight into prehistoric America. Elsewhere in the park are magnificent canyons and rivers.

Melting snows swell the cascading waters of the Rocky Mountain National Park. Four kinds of trout inhabit the network of streams and crystal-clear lakes within the park. Blue spruce and lodgepole pine rise from the riverbanks, while Engelmann spruce surrounds the higher streams.

Lowering clouds lend a threatening air to Battle Mountain, which towers to a height of 12,044 feet (3,670 m) above the Rocky Mountain National Park in Colorado. About one-third of the park is open mountainside, lying high above the swathes of dark green conifers.

Grand Lake entrance) and U.S. Highways 34/36 westward (for the Estes Park entrance). The park was inaugurated in 1915. This is classic Rockies country; snow-rimmed skylines soar to 13,000 feet (3,962 m) and over. Along a 35-mile stretch the great peaks rise above successive vegetation zones: tundra and alpine meadows, gilded with wildflowers when the winter snows have melted; Engelmann spruce and blue columbine; blue spruce, lodgepole pine, and aspen, with Indian paintbrush and pasqueflower; ponderosa pine and juniper. The crags are home to large numbers of bighorn sheep; during the rutting season, rams compete for favors by charging at each other headlong and smashing their heavy, curved horns together. Elk, mule deer, and coyote are also present, and marmots burrow in the high meadows. Keen-eyed hawks and eagles scour the high valleys for prey. Waterbirds, beavers, and trout inhabit the lakes and streams.

This section of the Rockies is archetypal Continental Divide geology, consisting of rock formations raised, after successive periods of upheaval, only 6 million or so years ago. In geographical terms this is very recent history, but subsequent erosion and glacial activity have left an indelible mark on this landscape. Moving ice has scooped out deep valleys over the ages, and glaciers are still at work in the park; no landscape is ever permanent. Many glacial and geological features may be observed from the park's 300 miles of trails. Fall is the most enjoyable time to tackle these. The views are wonderful, the air is clear and fresh. Permits are required if you intend to travel backcountry. The east and west of the park is linked by the highway, which takes one to trailheads, to the Alpine Visitor Center, and the scenic overlooks for Forest Canyon and Gore Range. The road's Trail Ridge section is closed by snow in winter. Southwest of the Moraine Park Visitor Center a road leads to Bear Lake, a trip well worth taking. The park attracts climbers, cross-country skiers, anglers, and horse riders. There are five campgrounds, which are very busy in the summer season. Hotel accommodation is available outside the park in local towns.

Bordering the Rocky Mountain National Park's southwestern corner are three great bodies of water: Grand Lake, Shadow Mountain Lake, and the dammed Lake Granby. From here the great Colorado River snakes its way southwest to the Utah line west of Grand Junction. To the south, 20,450 acres of canyonland form the **Colorado National Monument**. The red sandstone rocks have been eroded into caves and columns, such as the single tower of Independence Monument, 500 feet (152 m) high. The area can be seen to advantage from Rock Rim Drive, a 22-mile scenic loop of Colorado 340/Interstate 70.

In 1853 western Colorado was being surveyed by a team led by a Captain John W. Gunnison. They were attacked by Indians and Gunnison was killed; his name was given to a tributary of the Colorado

Gunnison country to the east of the Black Canyon, near Doyleville, Colorado. This magical landscape still retains the same power it held when Captain John Gunnison surveyed the region in 1853.

Overleaf: *The Cliff Palace Ruin at Mesa Verde National Park, Colorado, gives an idea of the building capabilities of the site's later settlers and their cultural achievements. The buildings blend in with the natural rockface.*

The Sun Temple at Mesa Verde, one of the nation's most important archeological sites. The Anasazi who lived here for over seven centuries clearly had a developed culture, but much of their lives remain a mystery to us. The Sun Temple, constructed in the shape of a D, was never completed; its ceremonial purpose remains unknown.

River. The Gunnison is a formidable river. It has bitten its way down into solid rock to a depth of 2,425 feet (740 m), forming the 55-mile-long Black Canyon. In some parts of the canyon the floor is only 40 feet (12 m) across. The sheer, dark cliffs loom menacingly on either side. The biggest is Painted Wall, a spectacular 2,250 feet (685 m) deep. The **Black Canyon of the Gunnison National Monument** (13,360 acres) protects a section of the chasm, and offers a chance to look down from awe-inspiring observation points. The North Rim has a graded road, closed by snow in winter. Access is easiest via the South Rim, and summer is the best season in which to visit. Camping is available, but permits are required for climbing down to the canyon floor. Colorado 347 off U.S. Highway 50 leads to the monument.

The southwestern corner of the state of Colorado is given over to Ute Indian reservations. Long before the Ute treated with settlers and prospectors in the nineteenth century, the southwest was occupied by another Indian people, known today as Anasazi ("ancient ones"). They settled the Mesa Verde region from about the sixth century A.D. to the thirteenth. Archeologists refer to the first settlers as "basketmakers." They farmed the mesa top, where they dug out their homes. Their descendants on the other hand built in the Pueblo style, raising huts of wattle and daub, and, later, of stone. During the last phase of the occupation they moved their dwellings to more defensive positions on the sides of the cliff. Some of these constructions have survived to this century, and in 1906 the **Mesa Verde National Park** was formed to protect them for posterity. Mesa Verde means "green table" in Spanish, and the park is set among 52,036 acres of typical southwestern plateau terrain. The 15-mile-long mesa rises high above the valley floor of Montezuma and Mancos. The cliff dwellings were suddenly abandoned about 600 years ago. We do not know why; perhaps drought drove their builders southward in search of a new home. The park is entered from U.S. Highway 160 between Cortez and Durango. A road leads south to the Far View Visitor Center (closed in winter) and to the many ruins. The most impressive site is the Cliff Palace.

The snows of the San Juan Mountains melt into the Rio Grande, which here starts its journey southward. Beyond lies the great arc of the Sangre de Cristo chain, curving south toward Santa Fe. The Sangre de Cristo is a barrier range of an unusual kind. Whereas most such ranges collect rain and snow from prevailing winds, these mountains collect sand. The sandy floor of the San Luis Valley is whipped up by the winds, and carried to the foot of the high mountain wall south of Cretstone Peak. The dunes rise in majestic sweeps to heights of up to 700 feet (213 m); with temperatures sometimes reaching 140°F (60°C) in the summer, one might be forgiven for thinking that the backdrop of snowy mountains is some Saharan mirage. When the sun is low in the sky, the shifting sands project a world of curving shadows and ripples and patterns of light. The area was declared the **Great Sand Dunes National Monument** in 1932. It covers 36,600 acres. Call at the visitor center for background information, for details of hiking, of the Montville Nature Trail, and of organized activities. Camping is available; accommodation may be found in Alamosa. Drivers should approach the national monument via Colorado 17, which links U.S. Highways 160 and 285 between Alamosa and Hot Mineral Springs. Turn onto Colorado 150 at Mosca.

To the north, halfway between Alamosa and Denver, is another national monument: The **Florissant Fossil Beds** are to be found off U.S. Highway 24, west of Colorado Springs on Interstate 25. They occupy 5,992 acres. This is an extraordinary site. Millions of years ago volcanic activity rearranged the landscape of the area swamping it with lava, ash, and mud. Rivers were blocked, and lakes formed. Subsequent geological activity resulted in the fossilization of a host of animals and plants: fish, birds, mammals, insects, and arachnids; seeds, leaves, and boles of ancient trees. Camping and accommodation is only available outside the monument area.

The Colorado-Wyoming line is crossed by the Park and Medicine Bow ranges. In southeast Wyoming the Laramie Range stretches northward to the North Platte River, beyond which lie the Rattlesnake and Big Horn mountains, which rise to 13,176 feet (4,016 m) at Cloud Peak. Westward across the Big Horn River are the giants of the central Rockies: the Wind River Range, of which Downs, Gannett, and Fremont are all over 13,000 feet (3,962 m), and the Absarokas, which skirt Yellowstone Lake. Wyoming's western border is fringed by the jagged peaks of the Teton, by the Gros Ventre, Wyoming, and Salt River mountain chains.

Over 8 million acres of national forestland are administered from

The driest part of Colorado is the San Luis Valley. Here, prevailing winds funnel sand toward the high wall of the Sangre de Cristo Mountains, and this piles up in large dunes. They are constantly shaped and reformed by the wind, forming ridges, crests, and crescents. In summer the dunes are golden, in winter white with snow. They are protected as the Great Sand Dunes National Monument.

Certain recognizable patterns recur frequently on the Great Sand Dunes. There are the bare ridges of sand known as "transverse" dunes; there are the sweeping "parabolic" dunes, partly stabilized by vegetation; and there are the "barchan" dunes, crescent-shaped shifting banks of sand. Call at the visitor center for a fascinating insight into the dynamics of this extraordinary natural feature.

Wyoming. The coniferous woodland of the high mountains form part of an ecological reservoir which is of national importance. In the west is the **Bridger-Teton National Forest** and the superlative **Shoshone**. In the south the discrete areas of the **Medicine Bow National Forest** include the Savage Run Wilderness. In the far north is the **Big Horn National Forest**, a land of lakes and alps which stirs memories of Indians on the warpath and tragic battles. East of the Powder River's south fork lie the **Thunder Basin National Grasslands**, 572,319 acres supporting eagles, deer, and pronghorn antelopes. The **National Elk Refuge**, near Jackson Hole, safeguards many wild creatures as well as the deer family; hawks and eagles are among the birds protected at the **Seedskadee National Wildlife Refuge** on the Green River.

Wyoming's most famous federally protected land is clearly that of the **Yellowstone National Park** (2,219,823 acres in the state's northwestern corner, overlapping Montana and Idaho). This huge reserve attracts visitors from all over the world. In the United States it is famous as the nation's first national park, created in 1872. The park's remarkable fauna was not protected until 22 years later. Today the wildlife includes cut-throat trout; ospreys and riverine bird species; ruminants such as bighorn, pronghorn, elk, and moose; the coyote; and the historically persecuted bison. Most famous of all of Yellowstone's inhabitants are its savage grizzlies and ambling black bears. Passing tourists offering them food have in the past been seriously injured. It should be noted that these are not tame and lovable cartoon characters, but dangerous wild creatures. Keep car windows wound up, do not approach them, keep camping rations away from your tent, and never attempt to feed them or any other wild creatures in the park. The national parks are not menageries, but some of the few remaining places in the world where large wild animals may live in their natural manner without human disturbance.

Yellowstone National Park is a natural amphitheater, a high plateau ringed by towering peaks such as Avalanche, Eagle, Saddle

Left: The Lower Falls of the Yellowstone River are a breathtaking sight, 122 feet (37 m) higher than Niagara as they plunge precipitously into the steep, pine-clad valley.

Below: Wyoming supports a variety of wildlife. Over 7,000 elk winter annually at Jackson Hole, under the Tetons. The National Elk Refuge is also home to a variety of other ruminants. Every spring the elk migrate northward, and in summer graze the high alps.

Mountain, Electric, Mount Holmes, and Sheridan. Mount Washburn is 10,243 feet (3,122 m) above sea level. The Yellowstone River rises in the south of the park, which it bisects on its journey north and east. In the south it forms the great expanse of Yellowstone Lake, which is flanked by three other large bodies of fresh water: Shoshone, Lewis, and Heart Lakes. The Continental Divide passes through the park. In the park you will find some unforgettable scenery. Pride of place must go to the Grand Canyon of the Yellowstone, best viewed from Artist Point or Inspiration Point. The river pours through a rocky channel 1,000 feet (305 m) deep and some 24 miles long, fringed by lodgepole pine and other brooding conifers. Two mighty drops are negotiated by the river en route: the Upper and Lower Falls. The latter is a thundering torrent of 308 feet (92 m).

Geologically speaking, the Yellowstone region has more in common with the Cascades Range than the Rockies, its landscape having been molded by volcanic action and by glaciation. After millions of years of activity, the volcanic upheavals are gradually calming down. This having been said, it is only too obvious that beneath one's feet the sulfurous inferno is still raging. This is evidenced by mudpots and hissing fumaroles. The park has about 3,000 hot springs and some 200 geysers – spouts of magma-heated water and steam which gush from fissures to heights of 130 feet (40 m) or so. Nowhere else in the world can match such a concentration of thermal activity. The most popular spectacles include the aptly named Old Faithful, along with Riverside, Castle, Grand, Grotto, and Giantess. The Norris Geyser Basin resembles a witches' cauldron, and Mammoth Hot Springs are building up new rock formations by depositing limestone in their pools.

Yellowstone has hundreds of miles of trails for the hiker, and offers an ideal introduction to the wild. Backcountry permits are necessary. Popular as the park is, its sheer size ensures the rambler the chance to communicate with nature in peace. Roads within the park form a great figure-of-eight, connected by radial roads with the park entrances. Winter closes most sections of these roads to any vehicles other than snowmobiles. Winter access is from the north only, to Mammoth; cross-country skiing reveals a snowscape shunned by many hibernating mammals, but beautiful and exhilarating. In season the park also offers riding, boating (with permission), fishing, and camping. Hotel accommodation is available within the park. Information about the park and its activities may be gained from the visitor centers. Summer visitors have a choice of five approach routes to the park: The south entrance is served by U.S. Highway 89/287; the west entrance by U.S. Highway 20/191; the north entrance (at Gardiner) by U.S. Highway 89; the northeast (at Silver Gate) by U.S. Highway 212; the east by U.S. Highways 16/14/20.

Yellowstone's southern neighbor is the **Grand Teton National Park,** whose 310,516 acres are linked by the John D. Rockefeller Jr. Memorial Parkway. Grand Teton may be approached from the east via U.S. Highways 26/287; from the south by U.S. Highway 187 from Hoback Junction; from the west via Idaho 31/33 and Wyoming 22. The Tetons are a small range in area, but are nonetheless most impressive. Ask a child to draw a snowy mountain, and the chances are that he or she will draw something very like Grand Teton. It is a towering, pointed peak which soars to 13,766 feet (4,196 m). Together with Owen, Teewinot, Moran, and the Middle and South Tetons, it forms a razor-crested horizon of jagged granite. Its winter face can be dour and menacing, or as pretty as a Christmas card. Under the blue skies of summer it is a natural wonderland waiting to be explored. The Tetons were created by a relatively recent upheaval along a fault in the earth's crust. One side of the fault reared up to form the range, exposing a wall of very ancient rock, while the other collapsed to form a valley. In the intervening ages erosion and glaciation have clawed the chain into its

It is easy to see how the Rocky Mountain bighorn got its name. Nearly 6 feet (1.8 m) from its white rump to its nose, and standing 3 1/2 feet (1 m) tall at the shoulder, its head is crowned with huge spiral horns. In the rutting season the rams charge at each other headlong, competing for the ewes.

A Yellowstone grizzly. The fiercest animal on the continent, a rearing grizzly bear stands nearly 9 feet (3 m) on its hindlegs. It weighs some 1200 pounds (545 kg). The name comes from the whitish tips to its fur, which gives it a grizzled look. It is generally larger than the black bears which are also found in Yellowstone, but the two are easily confused, as both species have variants in their coloring.

Grand Teton in early fall: The rocky peaks loom over the glowing colors of the valley. One of the first white men to explore the valley was John Colter, who left the returning Lewis and Clark expedition to explore the region in 1807–8.

Castle Geyser in the Yellowstone National Park, Wyoming. The hot springs and gushing spouts of water are one of the park's most popular attractions. They indicate that the volcanic eruptions which shaped this landscape are still, in geological terms, recent history.

present shape. The valley, known as Jackson's Hole, is crossed by the Snake River, which is naturally impeded so that is spills out to form Jackson Lake. The Teton region is home to elk, moose, and bighorn sheep, to bald eagles and trumpeter swans. Plant life includes blue columbine, penstemon, Indian paintbrush, quaking aspens, and stands of dark conifers below the timber line.

The Teton region was formerly a seasonal hunting ground for the Shoshone Indians, before nineteenth-century trappers came from the east in search of beaver pelts. The Grand Teton National Park was founded in 1929, and expanded in 1950. Today, many visitors come to climb (or learn to climb), to fish, or to go boating or rafting; permits are required for many of these activities. There are over 200 miles of trails within the park, which is ideal hiking and riding country. Highways cross the park, and a subsidiary road travels from park headquarters in Moose to the south end of Jackson Lake, via Jenny Lake. Call at the Moose or Colter Bay visitor centers for a full briefing on the park and its activities. Fall is the best time to explore the Tetons. In winter cross-country skiing expeditions are organized. Camping and other accommodation is sited within the park.

Wyoming not only has the nation's first national park, but the first national monument as well. President Theodore Roosevelt inaugurated the **Devil's Tower National Monument** in 1906. This extraordinary landmark is to be found in the northeast of the state, on the edge of the Black Hills of Dakota. Access is via Wyoming 110, a spur of Wyoming 24 (off U.S. Highway 14 from Interstate 90). The nearby town of Sundance is renowned in the lore of the Wild West as the haunt of Butch Cassidy and the Sundance Kid. To the Indians, Devil's Tower was known as *Mateo Tepee*, and was a place rich in legends. It continues to exercise our imaginations today: In the Spielberg movie *Close Encounters of the Third Kind* Devil's Tower was featured as the landing site of an alien spacecraft. The facts of this strange rock are almost as remarkable as its fiction. The flat-topped tower of furrowed stone is 867 feet (264 m) from top to bottom; its summit is 5,117 feet (1,560 m) above sea level. Its

The Grand Teton National Park was pieced together slowly. Local conservationists campaigned in the 1920s and in 1929 150 square miles of mountainside was set aside as a national park. During Franklin D. Roosevelt's presidency Jackson Hole was declared a national monument. Purchases by John D. Rockefeller completed the jigsaw, and in 1950 the park was expanded so that the whole area came under federal protection.

igneous rocks were formed underground over 1½ million years ago, and later exposed by the erosion of its sedimentary overlay. It was first scaled in 1893, its climbers building a giant ladder to cover the first half of the ascent. Today the monument takes in 1,347 acres and includes a section of the Belle Fourche River. There are 7 miles of hiking trails, and a chance to see prairie dogs, chipmunks, porcupine, and whitetailed deer. Beware of rattlesnakes. Camping is available not far from park headquarters, and a visitor center near the base of the great rock offers

information about the park, its history and wildlife, and organized activities.

The state of Idaho is dominated by the great bend of the Snake River and the broad swathe of its surrounding plain. To the southeast of the Snake lies peak country, cut by the river's tributaries. To the southeast a maze of creeks also drains into the Snake, before the great river turns northward along the Oregon border to plunge through Hells Canyon, whose depth is a record-breaking 5,500 feet (1,676 m). In central Idaho the Sawtooth, Lost River, and Lemhi ranges lead into the central massif of the Salmon River Mountains. North of the Salmon are the Clearwater Mountains, Nezperce Indian country. The north of the state forms a narrow "panhandle" around the lakes of Coeur d'Aleine and Pend Oreille.

Idaho is a wild state, whose terrain includes desert and wetlands, mountains and plains, canyons and buttes, barren volcanic wastelands, and lush, forested slopes. In the south of the state five national wildlife refuges preserve the habitat of waterfowl and waders, as well as that of whooping and sandhill cranes. In the far north the **Kootenai National Wildlife Refuge** supports bald eagles, ospreys, bears, and other typical creatures of the montane zone. National forestland is scattered throughout the southeast of the state. The conifers of the **Targhee National Forest** rise from cattle lands, and harbor grizzlies; its lakes and rivers support trumpeter swans. The **Sawtooth National Forest** includes

The great rocky stump of Devil's Tower, Wyoming, dominates the surrounding pine woods and grassland. Its volcanic walls are popular with climbers: Conditions must first be checked out with the park rangers.

"Craters of the Moon" seems a suitable name for this wilderness. And yet even among the volcanic desolation animals and plants are colonizing the cinder-strewn slopes. This fantastic national monument is in Idaho, in an area little known before 1921.

mountain country; Sun Valley is famous for its winter sports. Borah Peak (12,662 feet; 3,859 m) towers above **Challis National Forest**, which covers the Lost Rivers region. From the **Boise National Forest** northward, the Forest Service's 20-million-acre domain stretches northward almost uninterruptedly to Canada: **Payette, Salmon, Nezperce, Clearwater, Idaho Panhandle, Kaniksu**. The **Curlew National Grassland** in southeastern Idaho preserves a different kind of habitat.

To the north of the Snake River Plain lies the **Craters of the Moon National Monument**, founded in 1924. Its 53,545 acres really do resemble a lunar landscape, or perhaps some scorched battlefield. This is a lava bed, lying on the Great Rift; its black cones of cinders and rubble-strewn craters testify to the power of the volcanic activity which has repeatedly devastated the region. The lava flows have solidified into stony gray rivers and clusters of clinker; subterranean tubes have been formed, and dripping ice caves. Definitely a bleak and desolate place, yet this is not the psalmist's "valley of the shadow of death," for it has been colonized by hardy plant life and adopted by bird species such as the mountain bluebird. Human visitors should not be deterred either. The landscape is dramatic and fascinating. The visitor center tells the story of the region from its fiery origins to the present day. Camping is to be found at the monument; other accommodation should be sought in Arco or nearby towns. The park is situated on U.S. Highways 20/26/Alt 93.

Montana, as its name might suggest, lies athwart the northern United States' Rockies. Its highest peaks are in the south: the Absarokas, Madisons, Pioneers, and Anacondas. The Lewis Range stretches northward, culminating in high peaks near the Canadian border. The eastern watershed is drained by the headwaters of the mighty Missouri River system; formally designated the **Upper Missouri National Wild**

and Scenic River; it links up with the Yellowstone River just over the North Dakota line. Montana is at the head of the projected Continental Divide National Scenic Trail. It might take you half a year to walk to Mexico; for the less ambitious, Montana itself has no shortage of trails for backpackers or marvelous scenery. Many trails cross national forest-land, of which the state has over 16½ million acres, some of it virgin conifer forest rising from the slopes of snowy mountain ranges. Here are wild rapids and glaciers, waterfalls and lakes; here also are prairies, rolling hills, and broad river valleys.

The wildlife in these areas includes bighorn, pronghorn, mule deer, elk, wolves, coyotes, grizzlies, and foxes. Seven national wildlife refuges cater for the great flocks of migratory birds which pass through Montana. South of Fort Peck the dammed waters of the Missouri are surrounded by grassland and forest, and 1,094,000 acres of this has been set apart as the **Charles M. Russell National Wildlife Refuge**. Here the

varied habitat supports deer and a host of water creatures, as well as eagles and owls. In the west of the state, a **National Bison Range** has been created to encourage breeding stocks of this magnificent animal.

The conservation of the environment is a matter so important that it should extend over national boundaries. It rarely does, but Montana provides one exception. **Glacier National Park** (1,013,595 acres) is one of the last unspoiled fastnesses of the Rockies, which at this point straddle the Canadian border between British Columbia and Alberta. The Canadians created their Waterton Lakes National Park in 1895, and the Americans founded Glacier 15 years later. Frontiers are human creations, and this was recognized as early as 1932, when the two areas were formally united as the first international peace park, a symbol of cooperation. Glacier National Park is adjacent to Blackfoot Indian Reservation lands, and was in the past hunted by Indians of several tribes. Fur trappers from the east first ventured on their hunting runs in

Bighorn rams graze across the border, in Alberta. Glacier National Park joins with Canada's Waterton Lakes National Park to form an officially designated International Peace Park.

the eighteenth century; the landscape has changed little since those pioneer days.

The Rockies here are normally between 7,000 and 10,000 feet (say 2,125 and 3,050 m) above sea level. Kintla, Cleveland, Siveh, Jackson, and Stimson are even higher. The mountains of Glacier are the result of massive stresses in the earth's crust which occurred between 65 and 100 million years ago. One great layer of rocks was forced over another to create what is known to geologists as the Lewis Overthrust. Subsequent ice ages resulted in the landscape we see today, gouged by glaciers and honed by wind and water. Long lakes fill the cavities: the Watertons, on the Canadian border; Kintla, Bowman, Quartz, Logging, and Macdonald in the west; St. Mary, Sherburne, and the Two Medicines in the east. Some of the names are evocative of the past: Buffalo Woman, Beaver Woman, Gunsight, Medicine Grizzly, Mokowanis, Thunderbird. These icy waters reflect blue skies and gray rockfaces glistening with snow and ice; some mountains still groan under the weight of glaciers. Waterfalls and rivers abound. The St. Mary rises in the park and the north and middle forks of the Flathead form the park's southern boundary.

The ecology of Glacier is fascinating, as it represents the eastern

Lake Macdonald lies in the south of the Waterton-Glacier International Peace Park, near Glacier's west entrance. Going-to-the-Sun Road bounds its eastern shore, offering prospects of calm waters and misty mountain peaks.

extent of the Pacific zone, with such species as western hemlock and red cedar. The western slopes are moister than those of the east; forests are of larch, fir, spruce, and pine. The alpine flowers of summer are a delight, if shortlived. They include the gentian, the yellow columbine, the pink harebell, and the glacier lily. The eastern mountains descend into grassland, and here are geraniums, shooting star, and Indian paintbrush. Elk, moose, whitetailed deer and mule deer all live in the park, as well as mountain goats and bighorn sheep. The hoary marmot, beaver and otter are among smaller mammals. Bird species include forest birds such as Clark's nutcracker, river birds such as the water ouzel, and large predators such as the osprey and the endangered bald eagle. The park is famous for its bears, both brown and grizzly, which should be treated with due caution if encountered.

For the rider or the hiker, Glacier National Park offers some 700 miles of trails and a full range of camping facilities. Backcountry, backpackers require permits. Accommodation of a high standard is also available in the park, and is accessible via scenic roads, many of which are closed in the winter. The park is reached via U.S. Highways 2 or 89. The St. Mary Visitor Center is linked with the Logan Pass Visitor Center by Going-to-the-Sun Road.

The West

California, Nevada, Oregon, Washington

"The Coast" is how it is often referred to, as if there were no other. This reflects no arrogance on the part of the speaker. Rather it indicates the fascination that the Pacific coastline between Canada and Mexico holds for the rest of the world. It is a fascination which has over the centuries drawn settlers to the region in their millions.

Amerindian peoples were the first to arrive – hunters and gatherers attracted by the teeming rivers and forests, and by the ready supply of food from the sea. Varied cultures developed and thrived as more and more peoples thrust southward. Yurok, Tolowa, and Hupa Indians were among those who settled the northern regions, while Pomo, Salinan, Chumash, and Dieguno groups were among the southern coastal dwellers. Inland were Achomawis, Karoks, Yukis, Serranos, and many more. At one time over 100 groups existed in California alone, speaking a variety of languages and dialects. To the east the barren wastes of the Great Basin were more sparsely populated.

In the sixteenth century Spain and other European powers began to explore the Pacific, searching for gold and trade routes. The English seaman Sir Francis Drake passed through the Straits of Magellan in 1578, to harry Spanish galleons. The following year his tiny ship, the *Golden Hind*, made landfall on the California coast before returning home across the Pacific. In 1768 the Spanish, masters of Mexico, ordered the colonization of California, and this continued after Mexico achieved independence. Between 1769 and 1823 a series of Franciscan mission stations were set up between San Diego and Sonoma, linked by a highway, the Camino Real. The northwestern coast had in the meantime become the preserve of Russian, French, and British fur traders. A Spanish bid to settle Washington was made in 1791, but it failed. Nevertheless, the Lewis and Clark expedition of 1804–6 left no doubt that the Far West was indeed a second Eden.

The 1840s saw the birth of a new era. The first pioneers to travel overland on the Oregon Trail arrived in 1842. Washington was settled in 1845 and in 1846 California became independent of Mexico, to be followed by Nevada in 1848. California formally became one of the United States in 1850, Oregon in 1859, Nevada in 1864, and Washington in 1889. In 1848 gold was discovered near Sacramento and immigrants began to pour westward from the eastern seaboard of the United States, from Europe, and from China. Eleven years later gold and silver were discovered in Nevada as well.

The early years of the present century saw towns develop into huge cities and rural trails become highways. The Hollywood dream factory cast its magic glow over the whole west coast. This was a land of luxury and instant riches, in which the climate was pleasant and the land and seascape enchanting. For each generation, the dream was reinforced. This was a land for poets and artists, a land of inspiration and possibilities, a land for entrepreneurs, or a land of lotus-eaters, depending upon one's inclination.

Tumbling water in the North Cascades. The western slopes of the range catch the prevailing ocean winds, and the precipitation feeds a maze of mountain streams and waterfalls.

The landscape which exerted such magnetism deserved its reputation. From the rainy forests of Washington's Olympic Peninsula to the fog-shrouded Golden Gate, from the rocky tumble of Big Sur to the high surf of the southern beaches, the west coast is a land apart. This is literally true, for it is cut off from the hinterland by ranges of barrier mountains. The forested Coast Ranges stretch the length of Washington, Oregon, and California. They are backed by the snowy Cascades, which run south from Canada to California, and by the mighty Sierra Nevada on California's eastern border. These ranges shield the interior from the Pacific rains, so that Nevada, in the Great Basin, is largely arid.

The Far West is a land of contrasts, of wild rivers and high plateaux, of deserts and depressions, of sunny valleys famous for their farm produce, their vines, and their citrus fruits. However, despite its scented orange groves and its sleepy, sun-baked backcountry, the entire west coast nurses a terrible secret, which on occasion manifests itself in a cataclysmic fashion. It is an area of chronic geological instability. The San Andreas Fault, a deep subterranean fracture, passes through the region, causing landslides and earthquakes. In 1906 San Francisco was virtually destroyed in one such upheaval of elemental forces. Volcanic activity, pent up over the ages, periodically tears apart solid mountains and molds new landscapes. In 1980 Mount St. Helens, in Washington State, erupted in spectacular fury. The entire mountain top was blasted into the atmosphere, and vast tracts of countryside were devastated with ash and mud. **Mount St. Helens National Volcanic Monument** (110,000 acres), south of Spirit Lake on Washington 504, bears witness to this turmoil. Over the years, however, nature heals the scars, new trees seed and grow, and the deer and elk return.

Washington State's northernmost federal land is the **North Cascades National Park**, which was inaugurated in 1968. Flanked by the wildernesses of Pasayten and Glacier Peak, the park runs along the border with British Columbia. The long fingers of Ross Lake and Lake Chelan are incorporated within national recreation areas, and Ross, Diablo, and Gorge lakes are dammed for hydroelectric power. The main park is divided into a North and a South Unit. It is accessible via the marvelous scenery of the North Cascades Highway (Washington 20) and via Washington 542. Snow seals off the region during the winter months.

One of the best ways to view the North Cascades is from the air. The horizon presents great snarls of mountain peaks and dense forests looming from the mists. In the park are the summits of Spickard, Blum, Snowfield, Eldorado, and Logan. Goode Mountain towers 9,300 feet (2,835 m) above sea level. In the far north of the Ross Lake area is Hozomeem, celebrated in the writings of Jack Kerouac (1922–69), poet and one-time firewatcher for the Forest Service. His vivid sketches record the electric storms rolling across the brooding mountain. The North Cascades catch a high rainfall from the open ocean beyond Vancouver Island, and this has created a profusion of lakes and high waterfalls, as well as striking ice formations and a heavy snowfall. Some 300 glaciers are to be found within the park's boundaries, and it is past glacial activity that has carved out the deep valleys and lake beds. Away from the prevailing westerlies, however, the eastern mountain slopes are dry and sunny.

Summer is the time to explore the North Cascades, either on foot or on horseback. The trails pass through a fascinating variety of terrain, from high alp to pine forest, from meadow to scrub, and afford in places exhilarating views of the great peaks. The woods are the home of deer, moose, and black bears; sure-footed goats pick their way along the mountain ledges. Pacific salmon find their way up the Skagit River as they return to their breeding grounds, and are preyed upon by swooping bald eagles.

Primitive campsites are available for trekkers, but permits must be acquired for camping backcountry. Information is available from ranger stations and park offices. Sightseers may prefer to stay in Rockport, or,

Lupins cheer the slopes of Mount Rainier during the summer months. The high meadows of the alpine zone support other beautiful flowers as well, such as painted cups and Jacob's ladder.

make for Lake Chelan, in Stekehin, and drive over. Boating and trout fishing are popular pastimes, and the North Cascades attract many climbers. It should always be remembered that conditions can be harsh, and only experienced climbers should attempt the peaks.

The mountains extend southward from the national park area, stretching down toward the Columbia River. Southeast of Tacoma rises the most dramatic peak in the whole Cascades Range. At 14,410 feet (4,392 m), Mount Rainier is the highest point in Washington State and in clear conditions can be seen 100 miles away. It is surrounded by the 235,404 acres of the **Mount Rainier National Park**, which is accessible via Washington 706, Washington 410, and Washington 123 (off U.S. Highway 12). The mountain was named by English navigator Captain George Vancouver (c. 1758–98), who first sighted its peak from Puget Sound in 1792. No climber was recorded as conquering the summit until Van Trump's and Stevens' ascent in 1870. In 1899 the area was declared a national park.

Although belonging to the Cascades, Mount Rainier stands apart and aloof, a stunning mirage in the high clouds. Here again the moist ocean winds are converted into prodigious snowfalls. Over 90 feet (27 m) of snow can fall over the winter months. Twenty-seven glaciers grind their inexorable way down the mountainside, making Rainier the most glaciated peak outside Alaska. Mount Rainier, like Mount St. Helens, is a volcanic peak, thrown up amid violent eruptions. Its slumber was last interrupted a couple of centuries ago, but mudslides still occur and its internal heat is still sufficient to melt caverns and ponds in its ice-filled craters.

Rainier does not always present a harsh, angry face. Summer's melting snowlines reveal alpine flowers, lupins, and moss campion. Lower slopes offer grassy expanses carpeted with colorful wildflowers – gentians, lilies, and heathers. The base of the mountain rises from thick forest – a tangle of brambles, vine maple, yew, and Douglas fir. The

wildlife of the park is equally varied. Marmots and beavers are to be found, as are black bears, deer, mountain goats, and the formidable cougar.

The Park's Nisqually entrance in the southeast is open all year and leads to Longmire Visitor Center and Museum. Other centers are at Ohanapecosh and Sunrise. Snow makes most of the park's roads impassable during the winter. The popular Paradise Center on the Longmire Road offers tourists magnificent vistas and a base for exploring the trails, whether their interest is in the glaciers, the ice caves, or the flora and fauna of the mountain. There are seven campgrounds in the national park, but backcountry permits are required for the more intrepid explorers. Backpackers can hike around the mountain on a circular trail. Only experienced climbers should tackle the upper slopes. The less experienced have ample opportunity to learn the special skills of mountaineering under professional guidance. Skiing and snowshoeing are popular in winter.

Mount Rainier, the pride of Washington State and one of the finest peaks in the Americas. The mountain collects huge falls of snow and is famed for its many glaciers. Mount Rainier is volcanic, and capable of erupting at some point in the future. Thermal caves in the ice can provide an emergency bivouac for climbers.

Ferns and mosses abound in a temperate rainforest. This is the Olympic National Park, in Washington State. Here, the river valleys are green and lush, watered by rain-bearing winds from the Pacific. Trails climb from these through meadow and coniferous forest to the high mountain peaks.

Northwest of Mount Rainier another glaciated, mountainous region rises from dense woodlands. The **Olympic National Park** (908,720 acres), founded in 1938, is fringed by the 649,975 acres of the **Olympic National Forest.** These mountains have been thrust up by collision between two of the great plates which make up the Earth's crust. Inside the park are the peaks of Angeles, Carrie, Elk, Deception, and Constance; some 60 glaciers gradually grind down the contours that the earth has raised. Deep valleys, some filled by lakes, have been scoured out by glacial action. The principal peak is Mount Olympus (7,965 feet; 2,428 m), named appropriately after the home of the ancient Greek gods. Both national park and forest are skirted by U.S. Highway 101, the spurs of which penetrate the edges of the wilderness. Port Angeles is the site of the National Park headquarters and a visitor center; it is linked by ferry with Victoria, on Canada's Vancouver Island.

Thanks to the prevailing ocean winds, the Olympic Peninsula enjoys the highest rainfall in the continental United States. In any one year some 144 inches (366 cm) of rain can fall, mostly in the winter months. This has given rise to a most surprising and unusual phenomenon – a rainforest in a temperate climate. Ferns and hanging mosses abound, while Douglas firs, Sitka spruce, western red cedars, western hemlock, and black cottonwoods rise into the mists and gentle rains. These dank forests line the valleys of the Hoh, Queets, and Quinault. A visit to the Hoh Ranger Station offers a fascinating insight into this humid, green netherworld.

Ascending the western slopes, the vegetation changes to conifers and then to meadow and alpine tundra. Pay a visit to Hurricane Ridge (south from U.S. Highway 101) in July. The sunlit grasses are scattered with a profusion of wildflowers, glowing against the dark, folded valleys and the distant icy summits. The peaks themselves and the glaciers are popular with climbers, Olympus holding pride of place. For those who prefer backpacking, there is a marvelous network of park trails. The wildlife of the park includes the rare Roosevelt or Olympic elk, deer, and the black bear. Pacific salmon fight their way upriver in early fall, and otters also frequent the rivers and streams.

Washington's Olympic Peninsula is a place of many moods, of mysterious sea mists and booming breakers. The Pacific swell has shaped the coastline, forming caves, arches, and offshore islands. The long shore is backed by cliffs and forest, and is under the administration of the Olympic National Park.

Crater Lake and Wizard Island viewed from the southern rim. This was the site of an ancient volcano called Mount Mazama, which was active over 500,000 years before collapsing in a final burst of glory 6,800 years ago. Today, the still blue waters of the lake, once a secret place of the Klamath Indians, attract many visitors.

Many camping facilities are available in both the national park and the national forest, popular sites being at Fairholm, Heart o' the Hills, Hoh, and Sol Duc. Motels and tourist accommodation are to be found at Lake Crescent Lodge and Sol Duc Hot Springs. Storm King Visitor Center is closed in winter, but Hunter Ridge is accessible during this period. The park attracts skiers, anglers, swimmers, and riders.

The climate and ecology of the Olympic Peninsula depend upon the Pacific Ocean, so it is only appropriate that the national park also comprises a long, separate section of shoreline. It stretches from the Ozette Indian Reservation in the north to Quinault Indian Reservation in the south, taking in the Quillayute and Hoh reservations as well. Access is via the western loop of U.S. Highway 101, and a visitor center at Kalaloch welcomes summer visitors. The peninsula stands as a bulwark against the breakers of the Pacific, and offshore stand isolated rocky islands and stacks that have resisted erosion. Beachcombers can enjoy the bracing winds and explore the miniature world of the rockpool and its marine life. Offshore, seals and whales may be seen, and wheeling seabirds.

The extraordinary landscape of Crater Lake National Park. Conifers fringe the steep bluffs and evidence of volcanic activity abounds. The lake is overlooked by the summits of the Watchman, Llao Rock, Cloudcap, Mount Scott, Dutton Cliff, and Garfield Peak.

The bobcat is the wild lynx of the North American backwoods, a savage predator found in many of the western forests, such as Siskiyou. It hunts birds and rabbits.

Some 85 miles south of the Queets River is the estuary of the great Columbia River. This artery of the western ecological system, 1,200 miles long, runs through cliffs and gorges, creating waterfalls and peaceful creeks and backwaters. It also forms the state line: To the south lies Oregon, a lynchpin in the history of the Old West, and still a region of unspoiled natural beauty. Over half of Oregon comes under federal protection. The state has 14 areas set aside as national wildlife refuges, and these provide a haven for cranes, for birds of prey and waterfowl, for Columbian whitetailed deer and pronghorn antelopes, for mule deer, coyotes, and bobcats. As in Washington, the Cascade Mountains form a divide across the state, a watershed and region of high wilderness.

These peaks are traversed by the **Pacific Crest National Scenic Trail**, which runs an incredible 2,350 miles down the western ranges, and is a backpacker's delight. Passing through the wildernesses of Three Sisters and Diamond Peak, the trail runs south to **Crater Lake National Park**, whose 183,180 acres achieved their status as long ago as 1902. Motorists approach the park via Oregon 62 or 38, off U.S. Highway 97 north of Klamath Falls. From mid-June to mid-September accommodation is available inside the park at Rim Village. The northern park entrance and the circular Rim Road are closed by snow in winter. Nearby towns offer alternative accommodation.

Crater Lake is the deepest in the U.S.A. It occupies a 5-mile-wide "caldera" or imploded volcanic peak. This yawning cavity plunges below the water to a depth of 1,932 feet (589 m), and it encloses a new, smaller volcanic peak known as Wizard Island. This lightly forested cone of cinders rises from a dazzling expanse of water, which reflects the deep blue of the Oregon sky. The lake, which has long been held in awe by the Klamath Indians, was first discovered by white settlers in 1853, when a

prospector named John Wesley Hillman explored the rim. The national park area is typical of the Cascades: In winter months heavy snowfalls weigh down the branches of the fir and pine. The brief summer thaw sees yellow monkey flowers nodding in the breeze. The park is ranged by eagles and other predators, and in the forests ornithologists will spot the indigo feathers and jaunty crest of Steller's jay, and the pied tail of Clark's nutcracker. They will be luckier to see some of the park's other inhabitants, such as the Cascades red fox and the pine marten. Trail hikers within the park can enjoy fine views of the lake, as can drivers from vantage points on Rim Drive. Cleetwood Trail ends in a cove, and here one can join summer boat trips around the lake. Nature lovers should pay a visit to the Castle Crest Wildflower Garden.

With the exception of the sagebrush country of the **Crooked River National Grassland** (near Prineville), most Oregon land under federal protection is made up of coniferous forest, similar to that around Crater Lake. The Forest Service administers a dozen large units. Two of these are to be found in the southwest of the state. The **Rogue River National Forest** comprises 638,081 acres on the California border. Its Douglas firs and sugar pines descend from the flanks of the Cascades to overhang rocky cliffs. Backpackers can cross the heights of the forest by the Pacific Crest National Scenic Trail, but winter sports' enthusiasts will head for the slopes of Mount Ashland, off Interstate 5. The forest takes its name from the **Wild and Scenic Rogue River**, which carves its way through the forest on its journey from the Cascades to the ocean. The Rogue is famous for its white-water rapids, and for its steelhead trout and its Pacific salmon, which enter the Rogue at its Gold Beach estuary. The downstream section of the Rogue passes through the gorges of the beautiful **Siskiyou National Forest** (1,083,000 acres), where it is joined by its southern tributary, the Illinois River. This forest is of conifers and hardwoods, and the region is known for its rare orchids and lilies as well as the flowering shrub kalmiopsis. The latter has lent its name to the Kalmiopsis Wilderness, to the south. Forest dwellers include bear, deer, elk, and bobcats, and the many rivers within the forest are the home of otters and beavers. The Rogue is best explored by riverside trail or by boat, upstream from Gold Beach to Agness (U.S. Highway 101) or downstream from Grants Pass (Oregon 99 and Interstate 5). The rapids should be negotiated only by professional boatmen. White-water enthusiasts should also investigate other parts of Oregon: the **North Umpqua River** (Oregon 138 off Interstate 5), the **Deschutes River** in the north of the state, and the **Owyhee River Gorge** in the far southeast.

Traveling southward from Grants Pass on U.S. Highway 199, motorists should make a point of diverting east on Oregon 46 to visit the **Oregon Caves National Monument**. Covering 480 acres, the site features a number of extraordinary cave passages, which over the ages have been washed out of the rock by the water table. Amateur geologists should explore other Oregon sites as well, such as the igneous rocks of **Diamond Craters Natural Area** and **Glass Butte**, and the basalt cliffs of the **John Day River**. Three fossil beds in the John Day region together form a national monument.

Across Oregon's eastern state line, the landscapes of Nevada reflect its distance from the ocean and the effect of the barrier ranges to the west. This is a harsh and arid terrain for the most part, a combination of forested mountains and burning deserts, of wildernesses inhabited by the sage grouse, thrasher, and mourning dove. It is, nevertheless, a land of variety and strange beauty, which has more federally protected land than any other state of the Union.

Not many people go to Las Vegas for the view, but only 25 miles to the northwest along U.S. Highway 95 is the **Desert National Wildlife Refuge**, 1½ million acres of desert and mountain scenery. This is a stronghold of the bighorn sheep, and the wealth of bird life includes the magnificent golden eagle. West from Las Vegas on U.S. Highway 93 and Nevada 41 is an equally vast tract of land. The **Lake Mead National**

Recreation Area offers a more refreshing sight to the tired eye as it contains the brimming reservoirs created by the damming of the Colorado River, which straddle the state line with Arizona. The surrounding desert is impressive, and it deserves the respect of hikers who must be adequately prepared for the climate. There is ample accommodation and camping provision, and excellent recreational facilities.

Beauty is more than skin-deep at the **Lehman Caves National Monument,** a 640-acre site south of U.S. Highway 6, east of Ely. These beautiful natural caverns burrow far beneath the slopes of Wheeler Peak, an eerie underground wonderland. At 13,063 feet (3,981 m), Wheeler Peak towers above the sagebrush. Part of the **Humboldt National Forest,** the peak has one of Nevada's surviving stands of ancient bristlecone pines. The Humboldt Forests takes in a series of separate, widely spaced mountains supporting aspens and conifers. In between lie merciless expanses of desert. In central, southern, and western Nevada

Lassen Peak rises imposingly above the coniferous forest of the Lassen Volcanic National Park. It is hard to believe that it erupted violently less than 70 years ago, causing extensive devastation of the surrounding countryside. Thermal springs in the vicinity remind us today of the region's vulnerability.

the **Toiyabe National Forest** also comprises disparate areas and a wide range of vegetation zones. Its 3,374,432 acres include sagebrush scrub, and deserts, dense Sierra conifers, burnished canyons, and high plateaux.

The forests of California are very different indeed. The very fact of their existence represents a victory for the conservationists and serves as a reminder of the value of the national park system. Prior to the 1968 decision to preserve 106,000 acres of coastline as the **Redwood National Park,** the luxuriant forests of northern California were ruthlessly felled by commercial interests. They were worth preserving. Members of the redwood family were once found in many parts of the world. This was one of their last footholds, on the brink of the Pacific Ocean. The coast redwood (*Sequoia sempervirens*) is even taller than its bulkier cousin, the giant sequoia (*Sequoia gigantea*); it has a good claim to be the tallest tree in the world, and heights of 300 feet (91 m) are not uncommon. Some of these Californian giants first started growing over 2,000 years ago.

The park is approached by U.S. highways 101 and 199, and

Californian coast redwoods, dappled by summer sunlight. These giants tower above the Pacific at California's Redwood National Park and in Humboldt National Forest. The trees are probably the tallest in the world, and are extremely ancient.

Manzanita Lake is a popular summer camping ground and accommodation center for exploring the fascinating country around Lassen Peak. It lies at the northwestern entrance to the Lassen Volcanic National Park.

information is available from offices at Crescent City, Hiouchi, and Orick. Short trails lead one into the depths of the forest, a primeval world of filtered sunlight and woody scent. Mixed with the redwood are other plants: oak, alder, fir, madrone, rhododendron, huckleberry, woodrose, and sword fern. Elk inhabit this forest, and salmon and steelhead trout swim the rivers and creeks. Summer is the best time to come to Redwood, for the wet ocean climate brings heavy winter rains driving in from the coast. Summer is also a good time to explore the rockpools and shoreline of the 55-mile ocean stretch.

If Redwood is a testimonial to the struggle against human destructiveness, **Lassen Volcanic National Park**, to the southeast, shows how nature can come to terms with even more violent devastation. Lassen Peak, at the southern end of the Cascades Range, erupted repeatedly between 1914 and 1921. Lava engulfed the mountainside and laid waste the forests. Today, evidence of that eruption is still all around, and there are still many signs of volcanic activity: thermal springs, fumaroles, and vents. Nevertheless, the forest is doggedly re-establishing itself, and the 106,000 acres of park containing the 10,457-foot (3,187-m) peak are a naturalist's joy. The mountain is named after Peter Lassen, a trail guide during the wild days of the Gold Rush. The story is told that, despite his profession, Lassen had no sense of direction. One group of travelers became so irate with his aimless meanderings that they forced

Looking south along Point Reyes National Seashore, California: The Pacific Ocean swirls around offshore stacks. Beaches, dunes, and cliffs may be explored at leisure. Offshore waters are protected as a marine sanctuary.

him to climb the peak to get his bearings! A national park was established in the area in 1916.

California 44 and 49 lead to Lassen. Park headquarters are at Mineral, but accommodation and information is available at picturesque Manzanita Lake. Camping is strictly for the summer months, and permits are required backcountry. This is hiking and horseback territory. The **Pacific Crest National Scenic Trail** passes through the park, and the surrounding **Lassen National Forest** (1,060,003 acres) offers further scope for exploration and camping out; it includes the wildernesses of Caribou and Thousand Lakes. Wildflowers abound in Lassen, and include orchids, monkshood, lupins, and monkey flowers. The forests are of cedar, Douglas fir, white pine, cottonwood, and alder. Lakes and streams are the habitat of trout, salmon, chub, water ouzels, and kingfishers. Cascades' red foxes are natives of the region, as are chipmunks, mule deer, and Columbia blacktailed deer. The lakes offer sailing, swimming, and fishing; winter sports' followers enjoy the heavy winter snows typical of the Cascades.

California is a huge state, and between its northern and southern parts there is great diversity of climate and vegetation. **Point Reyes National Seashore**, 35 miles north of San Francisco, lies between these two worlds. An extraordinary raft of rock on the San Andreas Fault, this area of 70,000 acres was set aside in 1962. A peninsula, Point Reyes is

Tule elk: A cow and a young bull graze the inland pastures at Point Reyes. The close proximity of different habitats attracts abundant fauna: marine, and terrestrial.

almost cut off by the long inlet of Tomales Bay, ancestral home of the Miwok Indians. An old lighthouse marks the southwestern extremity; to the east is the broad sweep of Drake's Bay, the probable site of Sir Francis Drake's 1579 landing. The seashore is one of pounding surf and cliffs and caves, a world of fog and foam. Out to sea, sea lions play in the powerful ocean currents which in most places make swimming too dangerous for visitors. Inland are wooded hills and meadows, crossed by the hiking trails of Bear Valley. The national seashore is approached by the celebrated old coastal highway, California 1.

West of San Francisco, California 120 links Interstate 5 with U.S. Highway 395. This is the road to **Yosemite National Park**, which was first put under state protection in 1864, during the presidency of Abraham Lincoln. Its 760,917 acres cover the western slopes of the Sierra Nevada, greatest of the west coast barrier ranges. The great conservationist, Scots-born John Muir, first visited the wild Yosemite Valley in 1868, and was immediately inspired. His writings and his enthusiastic campaigning led to the creation of a national park in 1890, which took over the state park in 1906. Yosemite became famous throughout the world, and one of the most popular attractions in the United States. As the great cities have developed, so too the town-

Wildflowers and surf: the northern section of Point Reyes Beach in clear weather. This wild and bracing expanse of ocean shore is open to the elements: sea mist and rain, wind and sun.

dwellers' yearning for the wilderness has increased. Yosemite, so near to the great metropolitan centers, has faced a problem that is rapidly becoming common in other parts of the world: Interest in the region has grown to the point where the sheer number of visitors threatens the ecology of the park. Measures have been taken to limit the effects of tourism, but it is still best to avoid peak vacation times if you wish to enjoy the majesty of the Sierras in peace.

Yosemite is one of the most beautiful places on the continent. Its northern boundary is punctuated by a series of high, snow-capped peaks: Forsyth, Snow, Haystack, Acker, Quarry, Price, Mahan, and Bartlett. Creeks and lakes fill the valley floors. To the south are more snowy horizons: Clark, Red Peak, Moraine, and Buena Vista. The center of the park is dominated by Tuolumne Peak and the headwaters of the Tuolumne and Merced rivers.

The best-loved corner of the national park is without any doubt the Yosemite Valley, whose walls were cut from hard granite by the Merced River, and ground out by Ice Age glaciers around 8000 B.C. California 120 links with 41 at the valley's western end, and the roads loop into the 7-mile-long valley following both banks of the Merced. The valley walls rear up precipitously, 3,000 feet (914 m) high. They are guarded by the

El Capitan reaches a height of 7,569 feet (2,307 m) above sea level. This great tower of granite guards the northern flank of California's Yosemite Valley. El Capitan is an outcrop of very hard rock whose sheer face was cut by the erosive glaciation that enlarged the valley of the Merced River in ancient times. It is popular with climbers.

Left: Yosemite's North Dome stands reflected in the waters of the Merced. It rises four-square to the north of the valley wall. Yosemite National Park contains some of the most enchanting scenery in North America and has been popular since tourism first developed in the nineteenth century.

Below: Bridalveil Falls is 620 feet (189 m) high: only the third highest waterfall within the superlative confines of Yosemite, and yet twice the height of Yellowstone's Lower Falls. The best time to see the waterfalls is during the months of May and June.

domes of El Capitan to the north and Sentinel to the south. At the head of the valley, North Dome, Basket Dome, and Half Dome flank Tenaya Creek. From the wooded floor of Yosemite Valley the scale and grandeur of the cliffs are emphasized by a series of waterfalls. These are best viewed during the thaw, when the streams are in full spate. Bridalveil is 620 feet (189 m) high, and Ribbon is 1,612 feet (491 m). The Yosemite Falls is the king, the second-highest waterfall in the world. It plunges a total of 2,425 feet (739 m) from the rim, in two torrential cascades. Having explored the valley, take an overview by driving up to Glacier Point (in summer only) or climbing a trail, the Four-Mile or the Pohono. For an eagle's-eye view of the world below, climb to Sentinel or vertiginous Taft Point.

The center of the national park is traversed by the Tioga Road, closed by heavy snow in winter. Fifty-five miles west of Yosemite Valley are the Tuolumne Meadows, a swathe of high alpine grassland revealed by the melting snows. This peaceful, scenic area makes an ideal starting point for expeditions into the high Sierras. The southern entrance to the park, below Wawona, offers another attraction – the giant sequoias of Mariposa Grove. Yosemite has various types of accommodation available for visitors, from luxury hotel to campsite. Visitor centers provide a wealth of information about the region. Climbers must register, and backcountry permits are required. Riding, skiing, fishing, and swimming are popular, and naturalists are drawn to the park by its wildlife, which includes mule deer and bears.

A continuous belt of national forest stretches north from Yosemite to Mount Lassen: **Stanislaus, Toiyabe, Eldorado, Tahoe, Plumas,** and **Lassen** forests. To the south are the national forests of **Sierra** and **Sequoia**, and, to the west and south, **Inyo,** on the Nevada state line. John Muir would have been well satisfied by the achievements of the movement he started, and it is appropriate that the section of the Pacific Crests National Scenic Trail which leads south from Yosemite bears his name. The John Muir Trail passes the **Devil's Postpile National Monument,** a great rampart formed from colonnaded basaltic blocks, the result of ancient volcanic and glacial activity. Drivers can reach the rock by California 203, a western spur off U.S. Highway 395, and explore the surrounding forest, with its river, falls, and gorges.

The Muir Trail continues southward to **Kings Canyon National**

The Devils Postpile National Monument, California, is some 900 feet (274 m) long and 60 feet (18 m) high. Its basaltic rock formation is reminiscent of a great fence made of stone planks. From here, trails lead through coniferous forest to Rainbow Falls.

Park (460,136 acres) and its southern neighbor, the adjacent **Sequoia National Park** (403,023 acres). Kings Canyon, founded in 1940, takes its name from the headwaters of the Kings River, which rises northeast of Mount Pinchot, a peak of 13,495 feet (4,113 m). The breathtaking Sierras rise above gorges of the river which were cut deep into the rock by ancient glaciers. The southwestern corner of Kings Canyon was placed under protection as early as 1890, for it contains some of the biggest trees in the land, groves of the giant sequoia. The biggest of these is the "General Sherman," 280 feet (85 m) tall and with a base growth of 120 feet (37 m). Regularly blasted by lightning, the ancient "Sherman" remains as imperturbable as its historical namesake. Its pithy bark is about 2 feet (61 cm) thick. The giant sequoia may not be as *tall* as the coast redwood, but "General Sherman" remains the *biggest* living object in the world. Second place goes to a rival sequoia which has been nicknamed "General Grant."

It was to protect such marvels of nature from the rapaciousness of the logging industry that Sequoia National Park was set up in 1890, at the instigation of John Muir. It was the second such foundation in the U.S.A., and today the giant trees spread proud and tall. Perhaps the chief attraction of Sequoia National Park is another giant: the highest mountain in the United States south of Alaska. Mount Whitney has an altitude of 14,495 feet (4,418 m) above sea level, rising above the bleak plateaux and granite peaks of the high Sierras. Trails lead to the summit itself, threading through forests, meadows of wildflowers, lakes, and boulders. Within the two parks the different habitats sustain a varied fauna. Black bears, deer, mountain lions, and coyote live in the park, and the golden eagle hunts the high Sierras.

Both these national parks are very popular with visitors, and like Yosemite they can become crowded, although the farther reaches are strictly for backpackers. California 180 east of Fresno and 69 north of

Jeffrey pine overlooks the skyline of the high Sierras. Yosemite National Park contains tracts of wilderness and high mountain trails ideal for the backpacker. Advice should be sought from visitor centers or ranger stations before embarking on expeditions. The climbing is popular with experienced climbers from all over the world.

This beautiful trail leads to Zumwalt Meadows in Kings Canyon, California, following the south fork of the Kings River. The national park stretches southward from Glacier Divide to Sequoia National Park. It is bordered to the east by the Palisades and Split Mountain.

Visalia take one to Kings Canyon, while California 198 leads to Sequoia via Hammond. The scenic Generals' Highway takes motorists through the groves of big trees. Camping is available in both parks, and visitor centers offer information. Permits are required for backcountry camping.

West of Fresno the terrain drops to the San Joaquin Valley, along which Interstate 5 roars south to Los Angeles. Farther west is the southern section of the Coast Range. This is a world away from the high Sierras, yet even so there are fascinating places to explore. **Pinnacles National Monument** consists of 16,222 acres and lies on California 146 between U.S. Highway 10 at Soledad and California 25 north of San

Snow weighs down the branches in California's Sequoia National Park. The Giant Forest, shown here, lies in the west of the park area. To the east are high plateaux and the peak of Mount Whitney.

Giant sequoias line the Congress Trail in Kings Canyon National Park. The sequoia is a masterpiece of natural design. Its thick, soft bark protects the tree from forest fire, and it ensures its future by producing some 2,000 cones annually when mature. Its shallow roots spread out over a vast area. Some specimens are known to be over 2,000 years old.

Benito. The pinnacles in question are 1,000-feet (305-m) crags thrown up by ancient volcanic upheavals and eroded into spires. Hiking trails lead to caves and canyons, to the crags, and south to North Chalone Peak (3,305 feet; 1,007 m). Pines cling to ledges and trails wind through chaparral. Deer and gray fox inhabit the area, and the caves are occupied by bats. Camping is available. Access is either via the entrance station and Bear Gulch Visitor Center in the east or by Chaparral Station in the west. Spring is the ideal time to explore the Pinnacles.

Beyond the Coast Range are the Santa Lucia Mountains, a vanguard against the prevailing winds, and these descend to the magical shores of

Big Sur. California 1 hugs this coastline, winding to reveal a succession of rocky promontories and green hills, rolling waves and glistening sands. Sea otters, seals, and sea lions inhabit the coast, and whales sometimes may be seen offshore. Inland the Pfeiffer-Big Sur State Park offers trails through mixed forest. The **Los Padre National Forest** (1,752,583 acres) forms a backdrop to the Big Sur coast, and a large separate section covers the southern end of the Coast Range. This unspoiled forest of oak and pine is crossed by over 1,700 miles of trails, and if you are lucky you might see the very rare Californian condor wheeling high above. Once upon a time this huge black-and-white predator ranged the entire west coast. Nowadays, only 60 or so condors survive, protected in special sanctuaries. Ranger stations are to be found at Frazier Park, Ojai, King

Sequoia National Park, California: a study in soft reds and greens. A hollow sequoia looms through the upright ranks of timber.

California sea lions, a familiar sight off the shores of southern California. The Channel Islands National Marine Sanctuary protects the kelp-dense seabed of the Pacific and its island rockpools. These waters are visited by blue and gray whales, squid, Steller sea lions, and harbor seals, the beautiful Garibaldi fish and the comic brown pelican. The sanctuary, established in 1980, extends for six nautical miles off the coast of each of the Channel Islands.

City, Santa Barbara, and Santa Maria, and camping is allowed in permitted areas. Permits must be obtained for the wildernesses of San Rafael and Ventana.

The southwestern Californian coast enjoys a warm and balmy climate and delightful scenery, and this paradise has helped attract millions to the urban sprawl of Los Angeles, whose exhaust fumes create a smog that does little for the ecosystem of the region. Nevertheless, the 150,000 acres of the **Santa Monica Mountains National Recreation Area** make some amends, taking in sparkling beaches with swelling surf, wooded hills and valleys, groves of oak, and isolated cypresses. Due west of Santa Monica, separated from the coast by the waters of the Santa Barbara Channel, an archipelago of eight islands extends into the Pacific Ocean,

Mosses and lichens cover the rocks at Pinnacles National Monument, California. Live oak colonizes the fissures and canyons. The Pinnacles, eroded volcanic breccia, are set in a semi-arid chaparral zone on the San Andreas Fault. Camping, climbing, and day hiking are possible within the monument area; backcountry camping is forbidden in the interests of conservation.

Left: Guano whitens a rocky arch in the Channel Islands National Park. Western gulls, cormorants, and brown pelicans are among the hordes of pelagic birds which congregate here. Once the home of Chumash Indians, the islands have in their history been ranched, farmed, and served as a home to the U.S. Navy and Coastguard. The park was expanded to its present size in 1980.

Right: Death Valley, California, is a world of shimmering heat, desolate rock-strewn vistas, and abandoned mine-workings, relieved only by the color of a cactus flower. Death Valley has a special beauty, and may be explored by jeep or by a day's hiking.

Left: The magic of the Coast: Santa Monica beach turns to gold. The Santa Monica Mountains National Recreation Area includes beaches and wooded hills, enjoyed by the inhabitants of Los Angeles.

and this has been declared the **Channel Islands National Monument**, with a total area of 249,525 acres. Details of access should be obtained from the visitor center, which is on the mainland, at Ventura. Anacapa and Santa Barbara may by reached by boat during the daytime; permits are necessary for those intending to camp on these two islands, or visit a third accessible island, San Miguel. The islands have many unique features, and provide a breeding ground for marine birds and sea lions. The underwater world is equally fascinating, and ideal for scuba divers.

It is the marine climate of southern California which draws most vistors to the region, and yet the arid, sheltered zones of the southeast are just as remarkable in their own way. **Death Valley National Monument**'s 2,067,795 acres lie between the Funeral Mountains and the Panamint Range, a science-fiction landscape which stretches south along the Amargosa River. Once trekked by Indians and "forty-niners," Death Valley is inhospitable to say the least. It is a seething cauldron whose temperature has been known to rise to 134°F (57°C). The skyline

includes the 11,049-foot (3,368-m) heights of crumpled rock known as Telescope Peak, below which Badwater, the lowest point in the whole continent, sinks to 282 feet (86 m) below sea level. The valley includes vast tracts of sand dunes and baked rock, pans of salt and mud, buttes, canyons, and craters. And yet, despite the harshness of the landscape, Death Valley is undeniably beautiful. Its weathered rocks are variegated in strange colors and patterns, and the illumination of the searing sun can amaze the eye. Visit Zabriskie Point at dawn. The valley's name is inappropriate, for a host of creatures have adapted to life in the desert: insects, reptiles, rodents such as the kangaroo rat, named for its ability to jump, and predators such as kit foxes. The coyote can be heard howling by night, and it is during the cool hours of darkness that the desert really comes alive. Even the brackish water supports life, the little pupfish managing to eke out an existence in the creeks. Plant life also survives

Spectacular light effects are one of Death Valley's chief attractions. Dawn and sunset in turn transform the tracts of sand and rock into glowing panoramas.

The Joshua Tree National Monument marks the juncture of the Colorado and Mojave deserts. The trees themselves are easily identified by their array of spiky branches. The trees are home to nesting birds, termites, and the yucca night lizard.

despite the odds, by storing moisture in leaves and stems, or developing specialized root systems. Plants include cacti, mesquite, and, in spring, a variety of wildflowers.

Visitors should avoid the scorching summer temperatures if possible, and use their common sense. Always carry water and appropriate clothing, protection against the sun as well as warmth for the cool of the evening. All kinds of accommodation are available inside the national monument area, which is approached via California 190 (east from Panamint Springs, west from Death Valley Junction); 178 (north from Trona, west from Shoshone); and 127 (north from Baker on Interstate 15). Northeastern access is across the state line, via Arizona 58 and 72, off U.S. Highway 95.

Much of southeastern California is occupied by the barren wastes of the Mojave Desert, crossed by the ribbon of Interstate 40. The Bureau of

223

Manly Beacon from southwestern Death Valley. The bare rocks and folds seem to offer no hiding place, but a surprising number of animal species have adapted to this forbidding environment, most of them emerging in the cool of the night.

Land Management Office in Needles preserves 1,400,000 acres of typical desert, the **East Mojave National Scenic Area**. This wilderness includes mountains, caves, and vast stretches of dune. It is the home of desert bighorn sheep, mule deer, the plumed Gambel's quail, and tortoises. The vegetation varies from yucca trees and sagebrush to stands of juniper and pine. Hikers should be aware of desert trekking conditions.

Travelers from Los Angeles to Arizona on Interstate 10 experience a similar vista of rock and sand and cactus. The **Joshua Tree National Monument** (569,960 acres) lies between Interstate 10 and its northern fork, California 62, to the town of Joshua Tree. Headquarters are at Twentynine Palms, in the north. Roads lead south across the monument area to the southern visitor center at Cottonwood Springs. As always, hikers should come prepared for the desert and carry water bottles. Camping is available, and is best during the spring and fall. The national monument takes its name from a species of yucca which the Mormons are reputed to have called after Joshua, his arms upraised before the walls of Jericho. The shape of the branches has given rise to its alternative

The archetypal desert landscape of Joshua Tree is of great interest to geologists, being full of strange rock formations, hidden valleys, and stony outcrops.

nickname, the "praying tree." It grows to a height of 40 feet (12 m), and is found on high ground in the deserts of California and neighboring states. Many kinds of cactus are native to the area, and you should visit the Cholla Cactus Garden, which has a trail. Many of the monument's bird species nest in cactus; some prey upon the snakes and sun-loving lizards. Excursions in the park might include a drive to Salton View (5,185 feet; 1,580 m), to jumbled rocky valleys, once the haunt of Indians, robbers, cowboys, and prospectors, as well as to oases, the sites of ancient settlements. The Eagle Mountains skirt the eastern section of the national monument.

From the heights of the Joshua Tree National Monument one can look south to the Coachella Valley and a large depression in the desert landscape. In 1905 the Colorado River flooded this basin to create an inland sea. The **Salton Sea Wildlife Refuge**, one of the state's 15 federal sanctuaries, covers 35,484 acres at the southern end of these shallow waters. This is a home or stopover for thousands of waterfowl and waders.

The Pacific

Alaska, Hawaii

The United States may be a newcomer among the Pacific nations, but the political map confirms the extent of this country's involvement in the region. Far across the ocean lie the Trust Territory of the Pacific Islands, American Samoa, and the Unincorporated Territories (Johnston Atoll, Midway Islands, and Wake Island). Hawaii lies at the center of the ocean 2,090 nautical miles southwest of San Francisco, south of the Tropic of Cancer. It is the largest island of the Hawaiian Archipelago. The home of

a Polynesian people, the Hawaiian Islands were discovered by English navigator James Cook in 1778. Annexation by the U.S.A. occurred in 1898, and in 1959 Hawaii became the fiftieth state.

Their tropical climate and lush landscape set the Hawaiian Islands apart from the continental United States, and tourists flock to them in droves. Nevertheless, the volcanoes and forests, the white beaches and green valleys remain a delight, and two island areas now form national parks. Hawaii has a rich flora and fauna, including many species which are unique to the archipelago. Exotic blooms include the white hibiscus, the flame flower, and ohia lehua. Many birds feed on the abundant supply of nectar. The nene, a black-headed goose, was saved from extinction during the 1950s, by selective breeding programs.

The nene is thought to have evolved from the Canada goose, a migratory species of the distant north. The lintel of the American Pacific lies in those subarctic wastes. The peninsula of Alaska extends southward from the Point Barrow, on the Arctic Ocean, to the Gulf of Alaska. The narrow panhandle of the southeast comprises the Alexander Archipelago and the Coast Mountains, west of the Canadian Rockies. To the southeast, the long string of Aleutian Islands stretches out toward Asia. The interior of Alaska is a wild land of extremes. The Alaskan, Wrangell, and Chugach ranges include many of the continent's highest peaks. The arctic north is a bleak wilderness of ice, the realm of grizzly bear and wolf. Here the sun never sets in the height of summer; during the bitter

The Kodiak National Wildlife Refuge is an island in the Gulf of Alaska, and is a haven for eagles, seabirds, and spawning salmon. Its most famous inhabitants, however, are its enormous Kodiak bears. Male Kodiaks measure 8 feet (2.4 m) from nose to tail, and can weigh up to 1,175 pounds (533 kg).

winter the sun never rises. The endless expanses of tundra are inhospitable to humans, but support varieties of mosses, lichens, and other plants, thanks to the brief summer thaw. The tundra provides a summer breeding ground for a host of waterfowl, such as the arctic loon, a diver whose sad, unforgettable call is the most distinctive sound of the far north. Huge herds of caribou migrate across the tundra, swimming rivers and fleeing from wolves. To the south lies a dense belt of frozen lakes and swamps, with coniferous forests of larch and fir, the home of lynx, grizzly bears, beavers, and spruce grouse. Some western bird species of tit and bluethroat are really native to Siberia; the U.S.S.R. is only a short distance across the waters of the Bering Strait.

During the last Ice Age, nomadic Asian tribes crossed the Bering land bridge into the American continent, and came to people the length and breadth of the Americas. These were the first Amerindians, and the carved totem poles of their descendants may still be seen on the coast. Athapaskan speakers populated Alaska: Indians of the Tlingit, Tsimshian, and Haida nations. Other native Alaskans are also of Asian origin: the Eskimo, or Inuit, hunters of the Arctic Circle, and the island-dwelling Aleuts. Later settlements were by Russian trappers, and it was from its czarist neighbor that the United States purchased Alaska in 1867. Sceptics shook their heads at such a squandering of funds, but they were proved wrong. Timber, fishery, and mineral resources (particularly oil) paid dividends. Alaska became a full state in 1959.

Despite the advent of new towns and highways and oil pipelines, Alaska is still one of the world's last true wildernesses, a vast but sparsely populated area of outstanding beauty. Sixteen national wildlife refuges have been set up to protect many of the state's rarer creatures, such as the world's largest terrestrial carnivore, the Kodiak bear. Alaska contains one-third of all U.S. lands under federal protection. The going is often rough. Winter temperatures down to −50°F (−46°C) are enough to deter the most seasoned tourist, and insects can be an irritant in the summer, when the temperature can rise to a pleasant 60°F (16°C). The terrain is often more suited to snowmobiles and light aircraft than cars. Nevertheless, there are many wonderful attractions which are readily accessible, and for the seasoned backpacker or climber Alaska holds the ultimate challenge. However, one should always bear in mind that this environment will suffer from over-use or environmental abuse, and cooperate with the park authority in safeguarding the wilderness.

The northernmost land under federal protection is the **Noatak National Preserve**, of 6,559,000 acres. This wild region above the Arctic Circle is best visited by boat or plane. The preserve surrounds the winding path of the River Noatak, which drains the Brooks and Schwatka ranges. It reaches the sea north of the Baldwin Peninsula, and Kotzebue provides a base for exploration of this northerly region. To the south the Schwatka Mountains are drained by the Kobuk River, and 1,750,000 acres of its valley are protected as the **Kobuk Valley National Park**, best approached by boat or light aircraft. Journeys in this wilderness should be carefully planned; its wild beauty is best observed in spring or fall. Caribou and moose roam the park, and wolves and bears are among its more dangerous inhabitants. The vast hinterland adjacent to these two river basins forms the appropriately named **Gates of the Arctic National Park and Preserve** (8,473,000 acres). Although the majority of the park is open tundra, it also comprises tracts of forest and mountain, of river valleys and lakes, and these support a range of wild animals: grizzly and black bears, wolves, caribou, and Dall sheep. Take a summer flight from Fairbanks to Bettles, and then charter a light aircraft into the wilderness. Planes fly regularly between Bettles and Anaktuvak Pass. This is virgin territory, and mountain climbers or backpackers must rely on their own resources. There are no marked trails, and organized trips with a guide are to be recommended for the inexperienced. The valleys of the Noatak and Kubuk rivers have played an important part in the historical development of the Eskimo or Inuit peoples. A summer

A caribou displays its mighty antlers. The Alaskan tundra is a fragile habitat. Its herds of caribou subsist on minimal grazing, and migrate long distances in search of pasture. The caribou has played a crucial role in the traditional way of life of the Eskimo people, and more than any other creature it symbolizes the vast open wilderness that is Alaska.

Cross-country skiers explore the frozen wilderness of the Gates of the Arctic National Park, above the Arctic Circle. This vast preserve around the central Brooks Range is the domain of caribou and grizzlies. Spring is the best time for skiing; hikers prefer the brief summer, which lasts from mid-June to September.

Mount McKinley emerges from the clouds above the autumnal tundra in Denali National Park, Alaska. Its vertical relief is 18,000 feet (5,500 m) – and that betters Mount Everest's. Life on the tundra revolves around the brief arctic summer: Its plant life includes mosses, lichens, grasses, wildflowers, and dwarf shrubs.

flight northwest from Kotzebue to the **Cape Krusenstern National Monument** (658,000 acres) takes one to one of the most remarkable of Eskimo archeological sites, and a chance to see in the wild the creatures upon which these hardy peoples traditionally depended: seals, harpooned for meat; caribou, hunted with bows and arrows for food and hide; seabirds, once consumed whole. Eskimo lands also lie to the south across the Kotzebue Sound. The **Bering Land Bridge National Preserve** occupies 2,785,000 acres of the northern Seward Peninsula. The vestiges of the prehistoric link with continental Asia are also home to a fascinating variety of arctic fauna.

Southeast of the Seward Peninsula lies the Yukon River, a 2,300-mile waterway whose name will forever be associated with the wild prospecting days of the 1890s. Parallel mountain chains rise to the south: the Kaiyuh, the Kuskokwim, and the peerless Alaska Range, which surmounts the entire mountain system of the western continent. Here are the titans: Mount Brooks, Mount Hunter, Mount Russell, Mount Foraker (17,400 feet; 5,304 m), and Mount McKinley, an incredible 20,320 feet (6,194 m). This is the highest peak in North America, with a low snowline and an array of glaciers which inch down the mountainside like juggernauts. It takes its name from William McKinley, later president of the U.S.A., and can be seen 200 miles away. The Aleuts called the peak *Traleika*, the coastal Eskimos *Doleika*, but in the Athapaskan Indian language of the Kuskokwim dwellers it was *Denali*, "the great one." This is the name given today to the **Denali National Park and Preserve**, following the 1980 enlargement of the original Mount McKinley National Park (founded in 1917). Its 6,028,000 acres may be approached by Alaska 3 (north from Anchorage, south from Fairbanks), and in summer via Paxson and Cantwell along the rough but magnificently scenic Alaska 8 ("Denali Highway"). Access is also possible via railroad or with light aircraft. The park offers a variety of accommodation and campsites, and bus tours of the wilderness. Backcountry permits are required for more ambitious visitors; hiking is

Mount McKinley, clear in the September sunshine. North America's highest peak was thrust up by crustal movements along the Denali Fault. Its imposing skyline is hidden in clouds for much of the year. During winter, the temperature on McKinley's slopes can drop below −74°F (−70°C).

literally off the beaten track. For serious climbers the national park sets a number of challenges. McKinley itself, an ice-clad giant riven by crevasses and rumbled by avalanches, under a deep blue sky, rivals the Himalayas. The mountain forms part of the barrier against the prevailing ocean winds and so collects deep falls of soft snow. The park has a wealth of flora and fauna, witnessing annual migrations of birds and caribou. The grizzly bear roots for berries and small rodents, while wolves form packs on their hunting runs. The terrain takes in tundra and forests of conifers. Many creatures hibernate through the long winter months, and human visitors will also find the long daylight hours of the brief subarctic summer the most congenial period in which to explore the area.

Before the Mount McKinley region was thoroughly explored, most settlers in the northwestern wilderness assumed that the twin chains of Wrangell and St. Elias contained the continent's highest peaks. They were not very far wrong. Straddling the border with Canada's wild Yukon Territory are an impressive series of peaks: Wrangell, Blackburn, Sulzer, Bona, Logan (in Canada), and St. Elias (18,008 feet; 5,489 m). This high-altitude wilderness is enclosed within America's largest national park, the **Wrangell-St. Elias National Park and Preserve**. Its

Hubbard Glacier, in Alaska's Wrangell-St. Elias National Park. This park, at the meeting point between the Chugach, Wrangell and St. Elias ranges, is a great conglomeration of glaciers, mountain peaks, white-water rivers, and remote coastal strands.

13,188,000 acres border Canada's Kluane National Park, and together they form a preserve on a truly spectacular scale. The high ice spawns scores of gigantic glaciers such as the Malaspina, north of Yakutat. The river valleys too, such as the Chitina, are of glacial origin. Being larger than many small countries, the park includes a variety of features: tundra and coniferous forest, lakes and canyons and plateaux. The park is perhaps best explored by air, but it also attracts cross-country backpackers and mountain climbers, anglers and winter sports' enthusiasts. Primitive accommodation is available within the park. Motorists will find summer the best time to tackle Wrangell-St. Elias, and should approach the park via the road from Chitina to McCarthy, or from the north via Slana (south of Tok Junction on Alaska 1).

Few places in Alaska fit more perfectly the image one has of the frozen north than the **Glacier Bay National Park and Preserve** (3,234,000 acres). North of Icy Strait, the state's southeastern coastline is fragmented by 16 columns of ice which churn their way into the Pacific from the Fairweather Range. The sea here becomes dotted with icebergs as huge chunks of ice break free. Inland, the ice is receding; the park's fjords and forests and high alps are the home of a host of wild creatures.

Three Hole Point in Aialik Bay, on the Gulf of Alaska. The bay is one of the inlets making up Kenai Fjords National Park. This ragged coastline is home to bald eagles, puffins, and harbor seals. Offshore one can observe killer whales and Dall porpoises, as well as true whales such as the gray, minke, and humpback.

Riggs Glacier descends from the Takhinsha Mountains in the northeastern region of Glacier Bay National Park and Preserve. Light aircraft and boats are used for backcountry exploration of the Alaskan wilderness. These glaciers are the remnant of a minor period of glaciation which began some few thousand years ago. For the last two centuries the glaciers have been in retreat.

The seas are rich in fish and zooplankton, which attract large cetaceans and pinnipeds and thousands of squabbling seabirds. Glacier Bay is approached by boat or plane from Juneau; a bus links the Bartlett Cove campsite with Gustavus. Explore the bay in traditional manner by renting a kayak, but note that permits are required for all boats in these dangerous waters. The park operates a boat tour. To the north and south of the park, the panhandle is occupied by the country's largest forest. Tongass National Forest (16,832,727 acres) includes bog mosses, spruce, and western hemlock, the haunt of moose and bear.

Another 6,210,710 acres around the Gulf of Alaska are set aside as the **Chugach National Forest**. This is exhilarating mountain country, intersected by glaciers and fringed by a maze of fjords and islands. The North Pacific current sweeps northward to wash these shores with the Alaska Current; consequently the climate of Alaska's southern coast is mild and rainy. The **Kenai Fjords National Park** preserves some 669,000 acres of this environment of ice and sea inlets and protects its wildlife: sea

Lake Clark, 50 miles long, lies in the national park of the same name among Alaska's Chigmit Mountains. Its shores brim with icy water from the high peaks. Red salmon come here to spawn.

otters, sea lions, and seals, whales, and seabirds. Southeast along the Alaska Peninsula, the Aleutian Range forms a powerful backbone. These volcanic mountains have created an extraordinary terrain, which may be explored by taking a flight to the crater of the **Aniakchak National Monument and Preserve** southeast of Meshik (Port Heiden). To the north, separated from Kodiak Island by the Shelikof Strait, are the 4,093,000 acres of the **Katmai National Park and Preserve**. Approached by air, this volcanic wilderness presents a lonely expanse of snow and lava. Fumaroles give vent to the powerful subterranean energies. The famous Valley of Ten Thousand Smokes was blasted by a devastating eruption in 1912. Northward to Cook Inlet, and the high peaks of the Chigmit Mountains, **Lake Clark National Park and Preserve** (4,045,000 acres) is typical taiga country, with forest and bog, but also includes zones of high tundra vegetation. Caribou, Dall sheep, and bears roam this wilderness, which can only be reached by air. This is another volcanic region of outstanding beauty, but backpacking is for the experienced only.

Above: The Ukak River at the head of the Valley of Ten Thousand Smokes, Katmai National Park. In 1912 the Novarupta Volcano exploded in an eruption ten times as strong as that of Mount St. Helens. Its legacy was a land of steam and cracked rock, and from this the valley takes its graphic name.

Overleaf: Mauna Ulu lies to the southeast of Kilauea Crater in the Hawaii Volcanoes National Park. The park includes some of the Pacific's most extraordinary natural spectacles; it was established as a national park as early as 1916.

Right: A gateway to the center of the Earth: A vent in Hawaii's Kilauea Rift glows with elemental power. Volcanic activity continues to shape the Hawaiian Islands, and offers the visitor the ultimate fireworks display.

Despite its name, the Pacific Ocean includes many of the world's most restless volcanic areas. Far to the south of Alaska, the Hawaiian Islands owe their very existence to volcanoes that have thrust up from the ocean floor over the ages. The Hawaiian Ridge links two submarine ranges, the Emperor and the Mid-Pacific mountains. Hawaii, the "Big Island," has an area of 4,021 square miles and contains massive volcanic formations within its **Hawaii Volcanoes National Park**. Hilo (Hawaii) is linked by air with Honolulu (Oahu). The park's 229,000 acres are bisected by a stretch of Hawaii 11 between Pahala and Keaau; the southern coastline may be reached on Hawaii 130, past the black volcanic sands of Kalapana. The park is a tropical paradise of verdant rainforest, from which rise two active volcanoes. Mauna Loa (13,667 feet; 4,166 m) is in the northern sector of the park, and Kilauea Crater (4,079 feet; 1,243 m) is in the southern, reached by Crater Rim Drive from the park headquarters. Few places on earth afford such views of the volcanic inferno: bubbling trails of lava, cinders, pumice, and fiery eruptions. The activity of the crater is carefully monitored, to ensure that visitors gain the best views without being exposed to danger. Visitor centers are at Kilauea and Wahula.

Halona Point extends from the Kohlelepe Cliffs to Oahu Island, Hawaii, to challenge the Pacific. These rocks are the remnants of an ancient lava flow.

Maui, another product of magma, rises adjacent to the "Big Island," across the Alenuihaha Channel. Airports are at Kahului and Kaeeleku. Hawaii 37 and 377 lead to the 378 turn-off to **Haleakala National Park**. Primitive camping is available within the park's 28,655 acres, but most visitors stay outside the park in tourist accommodation. Haleakala Visitor Center is the place to call for an explanation of the geology and ecology of the park. *Halaeakala* means "house of the sun." It is a 10,022 feet (3,055 m) volcano, heavily eroded below the summit to form a crater-like valley, a desolation of pumice and stone, guarded by gaunt crags. The south of the park extends from the mountain slopes to the coast, and here the landscape is transformed into tropical rainforest which contrasts strangely with the uplands. The park contains many species of plant and animal unique to the Hawaiian Islands, such as the silversword and the nene.

The islands have many other areas outside the national parks which are of interest: Maui's Iao Valley, for example, or Kauai's Waimea Canyon. The cliffs of Kauai at Kilauea Point are protected as the breeding ground of pelagic birds. The fiftieth state plays an important role in the oceanic ecosystem, and is a gem among the archipelagos of the Pacific.

Sunrise dispels the mists over Haleakala Crater on Maui Island. Exotic plants have colonized other sections of the volcanic wilderness that forms the Haleakala National Park.

Overleaf: The beauty of the sunset across the Pacific at Honolulu, Hawaii.

The Nation's Natural Heritage

A state-by-state guide to federally protected areas

The following selection of federally protected areas offers a state-by-state guide to areas of interest. Many of them are featured in this book.

Alabama
Bon Secour National Wildlife Refuge
Choctaw National Wildlife Refuge
Conecuh National Forest
Eufaula National Wildlife Refuge
Russell Cave National Monument
Talladega National Forest
Tuskegee National Forest
Wheeler National Wildlife Refuge
William B. Bankhead National Forest

Alaska
Alaska Maritime National Wildlife Refuge
Alaska Peninsula National Wildlife Refuge
Aniakchak National Monument and Preserve
Arctic National Wildlife Refuge
Becharof National Wildlife Refuge
Bering Land Bridge National Preserve
Cape Krusenstern National Monument
Chugach National Forest
Denali National Park and Preserve
Gates of the Arctic National Park and Preserve
Glacier Bay National Park and Preserve
Innoko National Wildlife Refuge
Izembek National Wildlife Refuge
Kanuti National Wildlife Refuge
Katmai National Park and Preserve
Kenai Fjords National Park
Kenai National Wildlife Refuge
Kobuk Valley National Park
Kodiak National Wildlife Refuge
Koyukuk National Wildlife Refuge
Lake Clark National Park and Preserve
Noatak National Preserve
Nowitna National Wildlife Refuge
Selawik National Wildlife Refuge
Tetlin National Wildlife Refuge
Togiak National Wildlife Reserve
Tongass National Forest
White Mountain National Recreation Area
Wrangell-St. Elias National Park and Preserve
Yukon-Charley Rivers National Preserve
Yukon Delta National Wildlife Refuge

Yukon Flats National Wildlife Refuge

Arizona
Apache-Sitgreaves National Forest
Cabeza Prieta National Wildlife Refuge
Canyon de Chelly National Monument
Casa Grande National Monument
Chiricahua National Monument
Cibola National Wildlife Refuge
Coconino National Forest
Coronado National Forest (*also* New Mexico)
Glen Canyon National Recreation Area (*also* Utah)
Grand Canyon National Park
Havasu National Wildlife Refuge
Imperial National Wildlife Refuge
Kaibab National Forest
Kofa National Wildlife Refuge
Lake Mead National Recreation Area (*also* Nevada)
Montezuma Castle National Monument
Navajo National Monument
Organ Pipe Cactus National Monument
Petrified Forest National Park
Prescott National Forest
Saguaro National Monument
Sunset Crater National Monument
Tonto National Forest
Tonto National Monument
Tuzigoot National Monument
Walnut Canyon National Monument
Wupatki National Monument

Arkansas
Big Lake National Wildlife Refuge
Buffalo National River
Felsenthal National Wildlife Refuge
Holla Bend National Wildlife Refuge
Hot Springs National Park
Ouachita National Forest
Ozark National Forest
St. Francis National Forest
Wapanocca National Wildlife Refuge
White River National Wildlife Refuge

California
Angeles National Forest
Antioch Dunes National Wildlife Refuge
Cabrillo National Monument
Channel Islands National Park and Marine Sanctuary
Cibola National Wildlife Refuge

Clear Lake National Wildlife Refuge
Cleveland National Forest
Colusa National Wildlife Refuge
Death Valley National Monument
Delevan National Wildlife Refuge
Devils Postpile National Monument
East Mojave National Scenic Area
Eldorado National Forest
Golden Gate National Recreation Area
Inyo National Forest
Joshua Tree National Monument
Kern National Wildlife Refuge
Kesterson National Wildlife Refuge
King Range National Conservation Area
Kings Canyon National Park
Klamath National Forest
Klamath Basin National Wildlife Refuge
Lassen National Forest
Lassen Volcanic National Park
Lava Beds National Monument
Los Padres National Forest
Lower Klamath National Wildlife Refuge
Mendocino National Forest
Merced National Wildlife Refuge
Middle Fork of the Feather National Wild and Scenic River
Modoc National Forest
Modoc National Wildlife Refuge
Muir Woods National Monument
North Fork of the American National Wild and Scenic River
Pacific Crest National Scenic Trail
Pinnacles National Monument
Plumas National Forest
Point Reyes National Seashore
Redwood National Park
Rogue River National Forest
Sacramento National Wildlife Refuge
Salinas River Wildlife Management Area
Salton Sea National Wildlife Refuge
San Bernardino National Forest
San Francisco Bay National Wildlife Refuge
San Luis National Wildlife Refuge
San Pablo Bay National Wildlife Refuge
Santa Monica Mountains National Recreation Area
Sequoia National Forest
Sequoia National Park
Shasta-Trinity National Forest
Sierra National Forest
Siskiyou National Forest (*also* Oregon)
Six Rivers National Forest

Stanislaus National Forest
Sutter National Wildlife Refuge
Tahoe National Forest
Toiyabe National Forest (*also* Nevada)
Tule Lake National Wildlife Refuge
Whiskeytown-Shasta-Trinity National Recreation Area
Yosemite National Park

Colorado
Alamosa National Wildlife Refuge
Arapaho National Forest
Arapaho National Wildlife Refuge
Black Canyon of the Gunnison National Monument
Browns Park National Wildlife Refuge
Colorado National Monument
Continental Divide National Scenic Trail
Curecanti National Recreation Area
Dinosaur National Monument
Florissant Fossil Beds National Monument
Grand Mesa-Uncompahgre National Forest
Great Sand Dunes National Monument
Gunnison National Forest
Hovenweep National Monument
Manti-LaSal National Forest (*also* Utah)
Mesa Verde National Park
Monte Vista National Wildlife Refuge
Pawnee National Grassland
Pike National Forest
Rio Grande National Wild and Scenic River
Rio Grande National Forest
Rocky Mountains National Park
Roosevelt National Forest
Routt National Forest
San Isabel National Forest
San Juan National Forest
Shadow Mountain National Recreation Area
White River National Forest

Connecticut
Appalachian National Scenic Trail (*also* Maine, New Hampshire, Vermont, Massachusetts, Connecticut, New York, New Jersey, Pennsylvania, Maryland, West Virginia, Virginia, Tennessee, North Carolina and Georgia)
Salt Meadow National Wildlife Refuge

Delaware
Bombay Hook National Wildlife Refuge
Prime Hook National Wildlife Refuge

District of Columbia
Theodore Roosevelt Memorial Island

Florida
Apalachicola National Forest
Big Cypress National Preserve
Biscayne National Park
Canaveral National Seashore
Cedar Keys National Wildlife Refuge
Chassahowitzka National Wildlife Refuge
Egmont Key National Wildlife Refuge
Everglades National Park
Great White Heron National Wildlife Refuge
Gulf Islands National Seashore (*also* Mississippi)

Hobe Sound National Wildlife Refuge
J. N. "Ding" Darling National Wildlife Refuge
Key West National Wildlife Refuge
Lake Woodruff National Wildlife Refuge
Lower Suwanee National Wildlife Refuge
Loxahatchee National Wildlife Refuge
Merritt Island National Wildlife Refuge
National Key Deer Refuge
Ocala National Forest
Osceola National Forest
Pelican Island National Wildlife Refuge
St. Marks National Wildlife Refuge
St. Vincent National Wildlife Refuge

Georgia
Blackbeard Island National Wildlife Refuge
Chattahoochee National Forest
Chattahoochee River National Recreation Area
Chattooga National Wild and Scenic River
Cumberland Island National Seashore
Harris Neck National Wildlife Refuge
Ocmulgee National Monument
Oconee National Forest
Okefenokee National Wildlife Refuge
Piedmont National Wildlife Refuge
Savannah National Wildlife Refuge
Tybee National Wildlife Refuge

Hawaii
Haleakala National Park
Hawaii Volcanoes National Park

Idaho
Bear Lake National Wildlife Refuge
Bitterroot National Forest
Boise National Forest
Cache National Forest (*also* Utah)
Camas National Wildlife Refuge
Caribou National Forest
Challis National Forest
Clearwater National Forest
Craters of the Moon National Monument
Curlew National Grassland
Deer Flat National Wildlife Refuge
Grays Lake National Wildlife Refuge
Hells Canyon National Recreation Area (*also* Oregon)
Idaho Panhandle National Forest (*also* Montana)
Kootenai National Wildlife Refuge
Lower Salmon River
Lower Snake Wild and Scenic River (*also* Oregon)
Middle Fork of the Clearwater Wild and Scenic River
Minidoka National Wildlife Refuge
Nezperce National Forest
Payette National Forest
Rogue National Wild and Scenic River
St. Joe National Wild and Scenic River
Salmon National Forest
Salmon-Middle Fork Wild and Scenic River
Sawtooth National Forest and National Recreation Area
Targhee National Forest
Yellowstone National Park (*also* Wyoming)

Illinois
Chautauqua National Wildlife Refuge
Crab Orchard National Wildlife Refuge
Mark Twain National Wildlife Refuge (*also* Iowa *and* Missouri)
Shawnee National Forest

Indiana
Hoosier National Forest
Indiana Dunes National Lakeshore
Muscatuck National Wildlife Refuge

Iowa
Desoto National Wildlife Refuge
Effigy Mounds National Monument
Mark Twain National Wildlife Refuge (*also* Illinois and Missouri)
Union Slough National Wildlife Refuge
Upper Mississippi River National Wildlife and Fish Refuge (*also* Minnesota)

Kansas
Cimarron National Grassland
Flint Hills National Wildlife Refuge
Kirwin National Wildlife Refuge
Quivira National Wildlife Refuge

Kentucky
Big South Fork National River and National Recreation Area
Daniel Boone National Forest
Jefferson National Forest (*also* Virginia)
Mammoth Cave National Park
Reelfoot National Wildlife Refuge (*also* Tennessee)

Louisiana
Bogue Chitta National Wildlife Refuge
Breton National Wildlife Refuge
Catahoula National Wildlife Refuge
D'Arbonne National Wildlife Refuge
Delta-Breton National Wildlife Refuge
Jean Lafitte National Historical Park and Preserve
Kisatchie National Forest
Lacassine National Wildlife Refuge
Sabine National Wildlife Refuge
Tansas River National Wildlife Refuge
Upper Ouachita National Wildlife Refuge

Maine
Acadia National Park
Carlton Pond Waterfowl Production Area
Cross Island National Wildlife Refuge
Franklin Island National Wildlife Refuge
Moosehorn National Wildlife Refuge
Petit Manan National Wildlife Refuge
Rachel Carson National Wildlife Refuge
Roosevelt Campobello International Park (US-Canadian administration)
Saint Croix Island National Monument

Maryland
Assateague Island National Seashore
Baltimore-Washington Parkway
Blackwater National Wildlife Refuge
Catoctin Mountain Park
Chesapeake and Ohio Canal
Eastern Neck National Wildlife Refuge
Greenbelt Park
Piscataway Park

Massachusetts
Cape Cod National Seashore

Great Meadows National Wildlife Refuge
Monomoy National Wildlife Refuge
Nantucket National Wildlife Refuge
Oxbow National Wildlife Refuge
Parker River National Wildlife Refuge

Michigan
Hiawatha National Forest
Huron National Forest
Isle Royale National Park
Manistee National Forest
Ottawa National Forest
Père Marquette National Wild and Scenic River
Pictured Rocks National Lakeshore
Seney National Wildlife Refuge
Shiawassee National Wildlife Refuge
Sleeping Bear Dunes National Lakeshore

Minnesota
Agassiz National Wildlife Refuge
Big Stone National Wildlife Refuge
Chippewa National Forest
Lower St. Croix National Scenic River (also Wisconsin)
Minnesota Valley National Wildlife Refuge
Minnesota Wetlands Complex
Pipestone National Monument
Rice Lake National Wildlife Refuge
Sherburne National Wildlife Refuge
Superior National Forest
Tamarac National Wildlife Refuge
Upper Mississippi River National Wildlife and Fish Refuge
Voyageurs National Park

Mississippi
Bienville National Forest
Delta National Forest
DeSoto National Forest
Hillside National Wildlife Refuge
Holly Springs National Forest
Homochitto National Forest
Mathews Brake National Wildlife Refuge
Mississippi Sandhill Crane National Wildlife Refuge
Morgan Brake National Wildlife Refuge
Natchez Trace Parkway (also Tennessee and Alabama)
Noxubee National Wildlife Refuge
Panther Swamp National Wildlife Refuge
Tombigbee National Forest
Yazoo National Wildlife Refuge

Missouri
Eleven Point National Wild and Scenic River
Mark Twain National Forest
Mingo National Wildlife Refuge
Ozark National Scenic River
Squaw Creek National Wildlife Refuge
Swan Lake National Wildlife Refuge

Montana
Beaverhead National Forest
Benton Lake National Wildlife Refuge
Bighorn Canyon National Recreation Area
Bitterroot National Forest
Bowdoin National Wildlife Refuge
Charles M. Russell National Wildlife Refuge

Continental Divide National Scenic Trail (also Idaho, Wyoming, Colorado, and New Mexico)
Custer National Forest
Deerlodge National Forest
Flathead National Wild and Scenic River
Flathead National Forest
Gallatin National Forest
Glacier National Park
Helena National Forest
Kootenai National Forest
Lewis and Clark National Forest
Lolo National Forest
Medicine Lake National Wildlife Refuge
Metcalf National Wildlife Refuge
National Bison Range
Red Rock Lakes National Wildlife Refuge

Nebraska
Agate Fossil Beds National Monument
Crescent Lake National Wildlife Refuge
Fort Niobrara National Wildlife Refuge
Nebraska National Forest
Oglala National Grassland
Rainwater Basin Wetland Management District
Scotts Bluff National Monument
Valentine National Wildlife Refuge

Nevada
Black Rock Desert
Desert National Wildlife Range
Goshute Mountains (Wilderness Study Area)
Grimes Point Archeological Area
Hickison Petroglyph Recreation Site
Humboldt National Forest
Lake Mead National Recreation Area (also Arizona)
Lehman Caves National Monument
Lunar Crater Volcanic Field
Mount Grafton Wilderness Study Area
Pahranagat National Wildlife Refuge
Ruby Lake National Wildlife Refuge
Sheldon National Wildlife Refuge
Toiyabe National Forest

New Hampshire
Wapack National Wildlife Refuge
White Mountain National Forest (also Maine)

New Jersey
Barnegat National Wildlife Refuge
Brigantine National Wildlife Refuge
Great Swamp National Wildlife Refuge

New Mexico
Aztec Ruins National Monument
Bandelier National Monument
Bitter Lake National Wildlife Refuge
Bosque del Apache National Wildlife Refuge
Capulin Mountain National Monument
Carlsbad Caverns National Park
Carson National Forest
Chaco Culture National Historic Park
Cibola National Forest
El Morro National Monument
Gila Cliff Dwellings National Monument
Gila National Forest
Kiowa National Grassland
Las Vegas National Wildlife Refuge
Lincoln National Forest

Maxwell National Wildlife Refuge
Pecos National Monument
Salinas National Monument
Santa Fe National Forest
Three Rivers Petroglyph Site
White Sands National Monument

New York
Fire Island National Seashore
Gateway National Recreation Area (also New Jersey)
Iroquois National Wildlife Refuge
Montezuma National Wildlife Refuge
Morton National Wildlife Refuge
Oyster Bay National Wildlife Refuge
Target Rock National Wildlife Refuge

North Carolina
Cape Hatteras National Seashore
Cape Lookout National Seashore
Cedar Island National Wildlife Refuge
Croatan National Forest
Mackay Island National Wildlife Refuge
Mattamuskeet National Wildlife Refuge
Nantahala National Forest
Pea Island National Wildlife Refuge
Pee Dee National Wildlife Refuge
Pisgah National Forest
Pungo National Wildlife Refuge
Swanquarter National Wildlife Refuge
Uwharrie National Forest

North Dakota
Arrowwood National Wildlife Refuge
Audubon National Wildlife Refuge
Cedar River National Grassland
Des Lacs National Wildlife Refuge
J. Clark Salyer National Wildlife Refuge
Lake Alice National Wildlife Refuge
Lake Ilo National Wildlife Refuge
Little Missouri National Grassland
Long Lake National Wildlife Refuge
Lostwood National Wildlife Refuge
Sheyenne National Grassland
Sully's Hill Native Game Preserve
Tewaukon National Wildlife Refuge
Theodore Roosevelt National Park
Upper Souris National Wildlife Refuge

Ohio
Cuyahoga Valley National Recreation Area
Mound City Group National Monument
Ottawa National Wildlife Refuge
Wayne National Forest

Oklahoma
Black Kettle National Grassland
Chickasaw National Recreation Area
Optima National Wildlife Refuge
Salt Plains National Wildlife Refuge
Sequoyah National Wildlife Refuge
Tishomingo National Wildlife Refuge
Washita National Wildlife Refuge
Wichita Mountains National Wildlife Refuge

Oregon
Ankeny National Wildlife Refuge
Baskett Slough National Wildlife Refuge
Cape Meares National Wildlife Refuge
Cold Springs National Wildlife Refuge
Columbian Whitetailed Deer National Wildlife Refuge

Crater Lake National Park
Crooked River National Grassland
Deschutes National Forest
Fremont National Forest
Hart Mountain National Antelope Refuge
John Day Fossil Beds National Monument
John Day Wild and Scenic River
Klamath Forest National Wildlife Refuge
Lewis and Clark National Wildlife Refuge
McKay Creek National Wildlife Refuge
Malheur National Forest
Malheur National Wildlife Refuge
Mount Hood National Forest
Ochoco National Forest
Oregon Caves National Monument
Oregon Dunes National Recreation Area
Rogue National Wild and Scenic River
Rogue River National Forest (also California)
Siskiyou National Forest (also California)
Siuslaw National Forest
Umatilla National Forest
Umatilla National Wildlife Refuge
Umpqua National Forest
Upper Klamath National Wildlife Refuge
Wallowa-Whitman National Forest
Willamette National Forest
William L. Finley National Wildlife Refuge
Winema National Forest

Pennsylvania
Allegheny National Forest
Delaware Water Gap National Recreation Area (also New Jersey)
Erie National Wildlife Refuge

Rhode Island
Block Island National Wildlife Refuge
Ninigret National Wildlife Refuge
Sachuest Point National Wildlife Refuge
Trustom Pond National Wildlife Refuge

South Carolina
Cape Romain National Wildlife Refuge
Carolina Sandhills National Wildlife Refuge
Congaree Swamp National Monument
Francis Marion National Forest
Santee National Wildlife Refuge
Sumter National Forest

South Dakota
Badlands National Park
Black Hills National Forest
Buffalo Gap National Grassland
Fort Pierre National Grassland
Grand River National Grassland
Jewel Cave National Monument
Lacreek National Wildlife Refuge
Lake Andes National Wildlife Refuge
Sand Lake National Wildlife Refuge
Waubay National Wildlife Refuge
Wind Cave National Park

Tennessee
Big South Fork National River and National Recreation Area
Cherokee National Forest
Cross Creeks National Wildlife Refuge
Foothills Parkway
Great Smoky Mountains National Park
Hatchie National Wildlife Refuge
Lower Hatchie National Wildlife Refuge

Obed Wild and Scenic River
Reelfoot National Wildlife Refuge
Tennessee National Wildlife Refuge

Texas
Alibates Flint Quarries National Monument
Amistad National Recreation Area
Anahuac National Wildlife Refuge
Angelina National Forest
Aransas National Wildlife Refuge
Attwater Prairie Chicken National Wildlife Refuge
Big Bend National Park
Big Thicket National Preserve
Brazoria National Wildlife Refuge
Buffalo Lake National Wildlife Refuge
Caddo National Grassland
Davy Crockett National Fores
Guadalupe Mountains National Park
Hagerman National Wildlife Refuge
Laguna Atascosa National Wildlife Refuge
Lake Meredith National Recreation Area
Lyndon B. Johnson National Grassland
McClellan Creek National Grassland
McFaddin and Texas Point National Wildlife Refuge
Muleshoe National Wildlife Refuge
Padre Island National Seashore
Rita Blanca National Grassland
Sabine National Forest
Sam Houston National Forest
San Bernard National Wildlife Refuge
Santa Ana National Wildlife Refuge

Utah
Arches National Park
Ashley National Forest
Bear River Migratory Bird Refuge
Bonneville Salt Flats
Bryce Canyon National Park
Cache National Forest
Canyonlands National Park
Capitol Reef National Park
Cedar Breaks National Monument
Desolation and Gray Canyons of the Green River
Dixie National Forest
Fish Springs National Wildlife Refuge
Fishlake National Forest
Flaming Gorge National Recreation Area
Glen Canyon National Recreation Area (also Arizona)
Manti-LaSal National Forest (also Colorado)
Natural Bridges National Monument
Ouray National Wildlife Refuge
Rainbow Bridge National Monument
Timpanogos Cave National Monument
Uinta National Forest
Wasatch National Forest
Zion National Park

Vermont
Green Mountain National Forest
Missiquoi National Wildlife Refuge

Virginia
Back Bay National Wildlife Refuge
Blue Ridge Parkway (also North Carolina)
Chincoteague National Wildlife Refuge

George Washington National Forest
Great Dismal Swamp National Wildlife Refuge
Jefferson National Forest
Mason Neck National Wildlife Refuge
Mount Rogers National Recreation Area
Presquile National Wildlife Refuge
Prince William Forest Park
Shenandoah National Park

Washington
Columbia National Wildlife Refuge
Colville National Forest
Conboy Lake National Wildlife Refuge
Coulee Dam National Recreation Area
Dungeness National Wildlife Refuge
Gifford Pinchot National Forest
Lake Chelan National Recreation Area
McNary National Wildlife Refuge
Mount Baker-Snoqualmie National Forest
Mount Rainier National Park
Mount St. Helens National Volcanic Monument
Nisqually National Wildlife Refuge
North Cascades National Park
Okanogan National Forest
Olympic National Forest
Olympic National Park
Ridgefield National Wildlife Refuge
Ross Lake National Recreation Area
San Juan Islands National Wildlife Refuge
Skagit National Wild and Scenic River
Toppenish National Wildlife Refuge
Turnbull National Wildlife Refuge
Wenatchee National Forest
Willapa National Wildlife Refuge

West Virginia
Monongahela National Forest
New River Gorge (National River)
Spruce Knob-Seneca Rocks National Recreation Area

Wisconsin
Apostle Islands National Lakeshore
Chequamegon National Forest
Horicon National Wildlife Refuge
Ice Age National Scientific Reserve
Lower St. Croix National Scenic River
Necedah National Wildlife Refuge
Nicolet National Forest
St. Croix National Scenic River
Trempealeau National Wildlife Reserve
Upper Mississippi River National Wildlife and Fish Refuge
Wolf National Wild and Scenic River

Wyoming
Bighorn National Forest
Bridger-Teton National Forest
Devils Tower National Monument
Fossil Butte National Monument
Grand Teton National Park
Medicine Bow National Forest
Middle Fork of Powder River
National Elk Refuge
John D. Rockefeller, Jr., Memorial Parkway
Seedskadee National Wildlife Refuge
Shoshone National Forest
Thunder Basin National Grassland
Yellowstone National Park (also Idaho and Montana)